ACTING OUTSIDE THE LINES
Perilous Journeys in Pivotal Acting Scenes

Jack Forbes

JAFO PUBLISHING
375 Redondo Avenue
PMB 320
Long Beach, California 90814

ACTING OUTSIDE THE LINES
Perilous Journeys in Pivotal Acting Scenes

Copyright © 2011

ISBN 978-0-9836418-6-5

Published in the United States by
JAFO PUBLISHING.

All rights are reserved, but for permitted use by the U.S. Copyright Act of 1976. Copyrighted © no part of this publication may be distributed, reproduced, stored or transmitted in a retrieval system, or transmitted in any form without the prior written permission of the copyright owner.

Printed in the United States of America © 2011

Design & Typography: Redmond & Associates
M. Redmond — K. Thomas — R. Korns

Retouching: marioncreative@gmail.com
eBooks: rkorns@worthgold.com

Contact website information:
www.JafoPublishing.com

Table of Contents

Preface iv
Big League xiv
Celebration 10
Consensual Sex 20
Couple, The 28
False Witness 38
Inner Voice 46
Janitor, The 54
Letter, The 64
Municipal Complaint Department 72
No Money 80
Not Guilty 88
Passing Through 108
Prisoners 116
Private Eye 128
Prowler, The 132
Regular Guys 140
Ring, The 150
Road to Daisyville 158
Safe at Home 166
Second Chance 174
Seduction 180
Umbrella 188
Wiretap 198

Preface

IN THE SPRING OF 1984, I assembled a baseball team for the City of Long Beach, California, Sunday Baseball league. My cohorts in this venture were Joe Jennings (a hot pitcher recently out of USC baseball) and two of my high school friends Jerry Scanlan and Jeff Severson. We organized tryouts and put together a talented team. To the man, we were all serious competitors. The team was called, The Naturals, named for the movie of the same name, and we practiced every Tuesday and Thursday afternoon during the season. If a player missed a practice, he was benched by me for at least the first inning of the next Sunday's game. During the regular season we won every single game, and narrowly lost the playoff game between the "National" and "American" leagues of Sunday Baseball on a very controversial call. But that's another story. The point I'm making here is that our star shortstop, Jeff Severson, who was both an ardent athlete and fierce competitor, and who had played Defensive Safety over several years for various teams in the National Football League, consistently missed our Thursday afternoon practice. So, on Sunday, I'd bench him, and he'd bitch, and I'd put him in the game an inning or so into the game. This continued for most of the season, until *one day*...I thought about the fact that he loved baseball and that he literally hated not starting on Sunday. During that season, we all had girlfriends come out to watch the games, and Jeff often had more than one attend the same game, and *nothing* would stop him from making those Thursday evening practices...except for one thing: his acting class with Ivan Markota.

So one fateful day, I decided to go up to Hollywood with Jeff to see what this was all about.[1] Ivan's school, the Van Mar Academy of Television and Motion Picture Acting, was located on Santa Monica Boulevard in Hollywood, California in those days, and was right next to the Pussycat Theater where all the porn films of the day were exhibited. Across the street was a notorious sex shop where they sold, among other exotic products, ball crushers (I had no idea what they were and wasn't about to find out), but the real action took place inside Van Mar Academy. I walked inside and was introduced to Ivan by Jeff. Ivan gave me that toothy grin and welcomed me to his domain.[2] And make no mistake about it, this was *Ivan's* domain. He would regularly kick people out of the school for one perceived transgression or another and then, a few weeks later, graciously allow them back in "one last time," only to boot them out again later. Jeff himself seems to have the record for the number of times any actor was kicked out of Ivan's school. In any event, at Ivan's, kicking students out of school was a commonplace, widespread and continuing scenario. In fact, over the period of my first few years as an actor, I was kicked out of Ivan's school several times. On one of those occasions, I was given the boot for refusing to involuntarily donate to Ivan's "Christmas Fund." I told Ivan that if I wanted to make a "gift" to him, I'd make it because I *wanted* to, and not because I'm *told* to make it. However, even before I finished my impromptu speech in front of the rest of the actors, I had been kicked out of class. Anyway, back to my first day at Ivan's—what impressed me was the dedication of these young actors to their acting scene characters and to improving themselves as actors. I felt immediately comfortable with this eclectic group of thespians and decided to return the next week, and the next week and…

Within about six months of studying with Ivan (who had an uncanny knack for teaching the *business* of acting, among other acting skills), I auditioned for a show called "Divorce Court."[3] In those days, "Divorce Court" was using real lawyers for the lawyer roles. I found out where the casting director's offices were, walked in unannounced and asked to audition. I told them I had been a Deputy Public Defender for 4-plus years, was in private practice, studied acting with Ivan Markota and was a natural for this show. The casting director explained that normally auditions were on an appointment basis through agents, but they did need real lawyers. She decided that since I was already there, she would read me for an episode. With my background as a litigation attorney, the script was right in my wheelhouse. I was hired on the spot to be a lawyer in the episode of "Tucker vs. Tucker" and through that show, I earned the right to join SAG.[4] Shortly after that job, I landed my first Soap Opera acting job in an "Under Five" (basically, fewer than five lines in an AFTRA television show) on "Young and the Restless" as a nameless inebriated man at a bar. My one line in that episode was, "Sure, easy for *you*," at which time my character passed out. I was so worked up about being on a Soap Opera that when it came time to shoot the scene, in the first take, I actually blew the line! In the second take, thankfully, everything went well and my work was completed for that day. My study at Van Mar Academy marked the beginning of my professional acting career, but not the beginning of my *writing* career. That had to wait a few years.

My first attempt at writing an acting scene came when I studied acting at the Beverly Hills Playhouse. This was part of the late Milton Katselas' acting training, and my instructor at the time was the late Al Mancini. As an attorney in the Public Defender's Office in Orange County, California, I had seen a lot of private attorneys totally screw up their clients' defenses to criminal charges. So many lawyers took on criminal defense representations for no other reason than that it was easy money: there was no malpractice liability for attorney negligence unless the client could prove that he or she was actually innocent. As opposed to simply revealing a "reasonable doubt," actual innocence is very tough to prove. Hence, there were a lot of civil lawyers out of their element in criminal defense. So, I decided to write a scene for myself to perform in class where the criminal defense attorney was so incredibly incompetent that he was about to get his innocent client convicted of murder. *About to get* him convicted, because in the end, the Jury decides that enough is enough. The resulting scene, "Not Guilty," was from the heart, was in an area of my expertise (criminal defense, *not* incompetent lawyering) and was my very first foray into the world of writing for an acting scene or short film. In his critique of my acting, and of the scene itself, Al explained that watching this lawyer self-destruct had been, for him, like watching a snowball become an avalanche as it devastated a mountain slope![5]

After several more acting coaches, I still had the troubling problem of sporadically becoming nervous during auditions. This is a bad thing since casting directors are generally very busy and don't have time to bring actors in who cannot deliver believable readings. If the actor's performance is flawed by nervousness, it wastes the casting director's time and, if it's in a producer call-back, shows the casting director in a bad light. The concept of "burning bridges" comes to mind. Ivan Markota had taught his students to get rid of the nervousness by turning away from the casting director, director, writer and various producers at the top of the scene, hugging oneself, shaking once or twice violently and audibly exclaiming, *"Get off of me! Get the hell off me!"* Then, calmly, the actor was to turn around and do the scene. You can only imagine how *that* infamous routine was received in the casting community. I never did it outside of class.

Milton's teaching taught the actor to write down many things about the actor and the scene and "creative hiding," and subtext and to virtually pick apart each beat of the scene by intention and purpose and life goal. Through this process, the actor would know every step of the way and there would be nothing to be nervous about. Unfortunately, the over-intellectualizing of the acting process and compulsive preplanning of moves turned out to have major drawbacks and limited effectiveness, in my opinion. It turns out that life is *too complex* to plan out an actor's moves step-by-step in a believable fashion. But more to the point, at least for me, Milton's methods did not get rid of the *nervousness* I experienced from time to time in auditions. The nervousness I'm referring to is where my breath would be gone and my hands were slightly shaking and my vision was narrowed and my voice was faltering. Adrenaline would be surging and pumping through me and I couldn't figure out a way to stop it from striking at the most inopportune times.

In about 1993, the United States began permitting women soldiers to be assigned to combat zones throughout the world, and it crossed my mind that this policy could have some terrible unintended consequences. In this light, I wrote the one-act play, *Prisoners*, and it was produced at South Coast Repertory Theatre in "A Performance of New Works" on July 30 and 31, 1993. There was no particularly appropriate role for me in that play, however, but the performances by Leif Ekberg as A.J. and Danielle Hand as Julie were spot on.

Flash forward to about 2001. I went to Sonora, Mexico where they had a Club Med. It was a well-anticipated vacation and I was ready for girls, sports, dancing and fun! I arrived and I was amp'd for this getaway. My law practice had been going well, I had some money to spend, and I was ready for action. Early on the first day, I met a 20 year old girl, Allison Chance, who was a real live wire, a talented athlete and just a lot of fun. We played volleyball together, went sailing together, went swimming together and were both ready for a great week. We also had something in common: both of us were actors, and to top it off, Allison's mother was *an acting coach* in the San Fernando Valley. Allison contended that her mother, Bobbie Shaw Chance, was the best acting coach in Los Angeles, and that I should look her up some time. That time came sooner than I expected when late in the afternoon of my first day at Club Med I ran up the very hot sand from the water and managed to step down on a broken wine glass which someone had left buried in the sand. It cut one of my big toes down to the bone. After I was stitched up by an excellent Mexican doctor in Sonora, I packed my bags and returned to California

—my vacation coming to an abrupt end.[6]

When I returned to California, I decided to look Bobbie up, and almost immediately started studying with her at Expressions Unlimited in Sherman Oaks, California. Through these studies with Bobbie, I finally discovered the secret to avoiding nervousness. It had been right in front of me all those years, but I just hadn't recognized it. The "secret" was, simply, to understand the needs of the role himself, to understand what the scene is really about and to make a *commitment to be there for* and *to be there with the role*. Simple to say, difficult to do, but gradually, with Bobbie's help and after a lot of Saturday classes[7], I figured it out. Once I started studying with Bobbie I *never again* was nervous on an audition or in an acting role. Once I had made that informed commitment to the role, there was *no room* for nervousness because the "audition" was not about getting a job or being judged. It was about the *role*, in that life situation, period. But, *for purposes of the present book*, the real importance of Bobbie's class was neither her uncanny ability to develop truth in an actor's work, nor her quest to broaden an actor's emotional range; it was the **writing**.

When I started at Bobbie's Expressions Unlimited acting studio, *no one had been allowed* by Bobbie to bring in material they had written themselves for a scene for their own acting. Bobbie reasoned that you can write, and you can act, but you can't write and also act in a scene where you're a writer. She believed that the writer would get in the way of the actor when combining the two. I didn't buy it. I'd had success with Not Guilty (which was originally titled "Guilty by Default," now that I think of it), and I wasn't about to stop there. So after a few months at Bobbie's, I started writing scenes in which I would act. I would typically write the scene, bring it in, put it up, get some actor notes from Bobbie, modify the scene and bring it back in. This process would happen over and over until the scene clicked. Then, my scene partner and I would typically put it up on a Thursday night showcase for producers and other industry professionals. After several years of engaging in this process, I had written many and varied acting scenes, including a few which were repeatedly, and are still today, performed by other actors at Expressions Unlimited, including: Wiretap (renamed by Bobbie, "The Jack Forbes Scene"); Consensual Sex; No Money; Big League and Regular Guys. These scenes, in turn, helped me not only to progress as an actor, but also to transition into writing story ideas and treatments for television and film projects, and to writing television pilot scripts and feature film scripts as well.

I realized that over the course of my professional acting career, I had written a significant body of work in acting scenes, short films and one-act plays. These were works which I had not only authored, but, in many cases, cut my teeth on as an actor training in my profession. Eventually, I decided to make all of this material accessible to outside actors and to the general public.

So, as you read and enjoy ***ACTING OUTSIDE THE LINES—Perilous Journeys in Pivotal Acting Scenes***, I hope you can appreciate the events, encouragement and instruction which made it all possible. You're welcome to practice and develop your own acting with this material, but if you want to produce any of this in a short film or any commercial performance, you'll need to secure my advance permission in writing and pay a royalty. Fair enough? **Break a leg!**

Jack Forbes
Writer

---

[1] My interest in acting was not unprecedented in my family. My mother's Aunt Gertrude had been awarded a First Prize Gold Medal in the Home Declamatory Contest, for her rendition of "Wild Zingarella" in the Dramatic category at Chadron High School, Chadron, Nebraska on April 2, 1919. My mother Tottie had taken that a step further and was a professional dancer at Earl Carroll's world renowned theatre/restaurant *Vanities* ("THROUGH THESE PORTALS PASS THE MOST BEAUTIFUL GIRLS IN THE WORLD") in Hollywood in the early 1940s, and appeared as a dancer and

actor in many feature films of that era. Later, during my childhood in Long Beach, my mother performed in several plays at the Terrace Theatre and Long Beach Community Playhouse.

[2] This was my very first contact with the world of *professional acting*. Previously, I had taken an acting class in 10th grade at Woodrow Wilson High School in Long Beach, California. One of the scenes I did in this, my very first acting class, was from "Alice in Wonderland" where I played the Dormouse at the tea-party (*"No room! No room!"*). It is an absolutely hilarious scene and if you haven't read it lately, you really should read it soon. In any event, to my surprise at the time, after the scene was completed, the substitute teacher commented about how *impressed* she was (my first review!) with my work. She explained that I stayed in character as the Dormouse the entire scene and that she totally believed it. That was my very first acting role.

[3] You can find many of my credits as an actor at www.imdb.com by searching there for "Forbes, Jack (I)," or virtually all of my credits as an actor by simply visiting my own website at www.jafopublishing.com.

[4] There are a few professional actor unions in the United States. Generally, for film and most night time television, there is the Screen Actor's Guild or "SAG"; for daytime television, news programs and some cable shows there is the American Federation of Television and Radio Artists, or "AFTRA"; and for theatre performers, there is Actors Equity. AFTRA is an open union in the sense that anyone can join by simply paying the initiation fees. SAG and Actors Equity are closed unions where you need to qualify in some manner to be entitled to join. Recently, SAG and AFTRA merged into one union, SAG/AFTRA, a closed union.

[5] After another scene I did in that Intermediate class (a disastrous scene involving a fake beard and a decidedly phony English accent on my part), Al suggested I go to the beginner's class for a few weeks to study with Cal Bartlett (another of Milton's instructors). Instead of only a few weeks, I decided to stay with Cal for *six months* doing among other things, several scenes from David Mamet, before heading back up to Al's Intermediate class. I was not a Scientologist, and although Milton's classes were part of the Scientology movement, that was never pushed on anyone there. It was all about the work in class, the work in preparation for class and the necessity of *taking responsibility* for your commitment to acting.

[6] Club Med paid for all of my medical expenses and refunded all of my

money spent on the trip. After all, I may have been an actor, but I was also still a litigation attorney and knew my way around the block!

[7] Saturday classes were all about the actor, not the role. There, we tugged, pulled and pushed ourselves to open up our emotions and allow ourselves to be fully expressive without remorse, without reservation and without fear. Hence, the school's name—*Expressions Unlimited*. An actor can be natural, but if he or she is not capable of allowing emotions to be felt and experienced, the role may never be able to bring those emotions to bear and the actor's performance will fall short of reality. Although I continue to study with Bobbie from time to time, I'll always remember the many, many Saturday classes as enabling me to reach my potential as an actor.

Big League

IN A BASEBALL LOCKER ROOM – a *battered baseball player, JOHNNY McCLURE, late 20s, storms in, slamming his glove down and pacing as he rants.*

McCLURE: Throw me out and I don't give a shit. Fucked-up umpire. *(simulates the ensuing bench emptying brawl)* Nobody gets to me. Baamm! Get offa me. Nobody gets a piece.

This goes on for several seconds while McClure re-lives the brawl following his beaning a batter with a fast-ball pitch. McClure slows down, exhausted.

McCLURE: They started this last fucking night. ... Shouldn't of made me do that. Hit that fucker...Hit that...guy in the face like...I hit him in the face...Oh, fuck me. ... I never thought I'd get him in the face.

McClure is crying. TOMMY HOPPER, the team Manager, walks in from the hallway. He's been listening to this go down.

TOMMY: He's not too good, but they got him in the ambulance. McClure, you hear me?

McClure's in a daze, head in hands.

TOMMY: Vitals are okay. Got a call from the team owner...

McCLURE: *(not really buying it)* He'll be alright?

TOMMY: *(not convinced himself)* Oh yeah.

McCLURE: He wasn't moving.

TOMMY: I know.

McCLURE: I kept gettin' slugged but I could see Jimmy Baker.

TOMMY: Medics got there quick.

McCLURE: Fuckers kept hittin' me, 'til our guys...

TOMMY: Whole bench emptied out...Even Rueben for god's sake.

McCLURE: Yeah?

TOMMY: Charge in outta left field. If he could only run that fast for a hit ball.

McCLURE: *(laughs)* The man needs a new set of wheels. ... He came in for me?

TOMMY: On a flier he did.

McCLURE: A good guy. Doesn't speak a word of English, but he's okay.

TOMMY: And Johnson got a shiner.

McCLURE: Tommy Johnson?

TOMMY: Tommy, yeah. A shiner, but we got our licks in, believe me.

McCLURE: We did?

TOMMY: Bet your ass.

McCLURE: Good, they deserved it. Fuck them.

TOMMY: Came up pretty hard.

McCLURE: Rising fastball...

TOMMY: High and tight, and that's not...

McCLURE: In the face, Tommy. I hit him in the face.

TOMMY: And that's not the way...

McCLURE: And I'm messed up Coach, 'cause I see him lyin' there, people around, but he's not movin'. They're screamin' "Medic, medic!"

TOMMY: Johnny, now just slow down.

McCLURE: Guys beatin' on me, but Jimmy Baker's still not movin'.

TOMMY: Okay, settle...

McCLURE: I see him, and, you know, this is really fuckin' with my head...

TOMMY: McClure, hey! So you're not the one in the ambulance, so snap outta this shit.

McCLURE: What?

TOMMY: You threw the ball, you take the consequences.

McCLURE: You told me to make the throw. You gave the sign.

TOMMY: To hit him in the back. You go for the back, his side. He gives you his side, his arm. That's what ball players do. You don't throw for the head.

McCLURE: That's not what the pitching coach...

TOMMY: I don't wanna hear it.

McCLURE: Benny Rodriguez, the team pitching coach...

TOMMY: And I don't give a shit about the pitching coach said, and I deal with him, believe-fucking-me.

McCLURE: He said the helmet...

TOMMY: That's not the...

McCLURE: Coach, he TOLD ME before.

TOMMY: He told you, fine, but you got the ball, Johnny McClure, and nobody else. The fucking BUCK stops with you.

McCLURE: *(flatly)* You gave the sign.

TOMMY: And you go for his back, everybody knows that! Frank's on the D.L. six weeks while his god damned elbow heals from last night's fiasco, and the Padres should motherfucking know, expect I'd give the sign. So fuck them.

McCLURE: I hurt him bad.

TOMMY: And he'll make it. They always make it. A little time out, he'll be back. And maybe they think twice next time.

McCLURE: Why didn't he turn, hit the helmet, anything? I'm so sorry.

TOMMY: Well don't get too sorry, 'cause a few of our guys got tossed.

McCLURE: From the game?

TOMMY: Four of our guys, plus you, so that makes six.

McCLURE: A Padres player too?

TOMMY: No, shit no. Five of their guys. Like two-thirds their starters.

McCLURE: Two-thirds! No shit. ... Then who's the sixth, our guys?

TOMMY: Me.

McCLURE: *(surprised, confused)* You got in the brawl, Tommy?

TOMMY: No.

McCLURE: They why'd you...

TOMMY: I'm into the Blue. I knew you...Let's say I assumed you wouldn't throw a fuckin' bean ball. So I tell the Blue, "It's a slip."

McCLURE: But you gave the...

TOMMY: Sign, right, and I just said what the sign means... But, are you listening? I went to bat for you.

McCLURE: I didn't know.

TOMMY: *(re-living it)* "I don't care ten of my guys were hit yesterday. The god damned ball slipped."

McCLURE: You told him?

TOMMY: "A muggy night, the ball gets greasy and that's it."

McCLURE: A muggy night?

TOMMY: "The ball got away."

McCLURE: He's hearing this.

TOMMY: Watch it in the news.

McCLURE: I'm gonna watch it.

TOMMY: "Well you don't know your ass from second base!"

McCLURE: Holy shit! Your ass from second base? Holy shit.

TOMMY: Oh yeah. That's when he threw me out.

McCLURE: You're in trouble now. Coach, you're hip deep in the shit-house now.

TOMMY: "You want a non-contact game, **take up tiddly-winks**!"

McCLURE: I gotta see it.

TOMMY: I couldn't believe it myself when that came outta my mouth. Tiddly-winks.

McCLURE: I love it.

TOMMY: Ten o'clock news.

McCLURE: Okay, okay I will.

TOMMY: So now I got three Blues screamin' my face "leave the field, leave the field!" Security-fucking-police walking out.

McCLURE: It wasn't a home game, we'd had the fans on our ass.

TOMMY: That's a fact.

McCLURE: I'm on the ground, gettin' the shit beat outta me, and you're bringin' it to the Blue. That's so fuckin' great. Tommy Hopper, out there takin' the heat. You know, it's been a long time since anybody's stuck their neck out for me like that.

TOMMY: If I don't protect my guys, who's gonna do it? I got your back.

McCLURE: "Team play," it's always been a lot of talk. But you and the guys came through. That's Big League. That's what its all about. Thanks, coach.

TOMMY: *(pause)* Yeah, well, don't cuddle up just yet. League's after your ass.

McCLURE: Suspension?

TOMMY: Ten games, minimum.

McCLURE: Loss of pay?

TOMMY: You know the drill.

McCLURE: *(slight smile)* Looks like some down-time for the Kid.

TOMMY: Now, you need to listen to me. Nobody throws for the head, not in my organization. The head-hunting days of Don-fucking-Drysdale are long gone.

McCLURE: Keep it on the down-low...

TOMMY: I give the sign, you throw for the back, for the hip, for the leg.

McCLURE: *(lightly)* I'm goin' for the shin. No, the ankles.

TOMMY: Don't get smart. You brush back at the numbers. You don't throw to the head, the neck, the shoulders, flat-fucking-period.

McCLURE: *(salutes)* Loud and clear.

TOMMY: If it happens again – Okay, you get the idea.

McCLURE: Right.

Tommy starts to leave.

TOMMY: And the pitching coach is on my shit-list for a little tete-a-fucking-tete with him momentarily.

The phone rings. Tommy picks up and listens.

TOMMY: *(to the phone)* Yeah? ... Yeah...I see. Alright.

McClure looks on, worried, expecting the worst. Tommy looks over at him. It doesn't look good.

TOMMY: I'll tell him. *(to McClure)* Baker woke up at the hospital. Left cheekbone's fractured, but no head injuries, so that's good. He's gonna be alright.

McClure's up and hugging Tommy.

McCLURE: Oh, that's great news. I'm so happy. I was worried, you know.

TOMMY: Yeah, yeah.

McCLURE: You think I could visit?

TOMMY: *(breaks away)* Let's not go fucking overboard. Just shower up. You're stinkin' to high heaven and got blood all over your god damned face. I'll see you at practice before tomorrow's game.

Tommy walks out. Johnny glances around for his ball and glove. He walks over, picks them up and works the ball with his hands. He puts on his glove and throws a few into the pocket. Johnny's back.

Celebration

INSIDE AN APARTMENT – *BILL, late 20s to 30s, lets a police DETECTIVE into his apartment. Detective holds a manila envelope and a note pad and has a pen, a holstered gun, a pocket recorder, badge and handcuffs. Bill appears distraught.*

DETECTIVE: Sorry for dropping in like this. How are you holding up?

BILL: It's been pretty tough.

They walk over to a table and sit across from each other.

DETECTIVE: I can understand that.

BILL: No, I mean I'm in pretty bad shape.

DETECTIVE: You'll get better.

BILL: That's what they say.

DETECTIVE: I could come back later, tomorrow maybe.

BILL: No, it's okay.

The Detective opens the envelope, but doesn't reveal the contents. Detective takes out and starts his tape recorder.

DETECTIVE: The lab sent these to me. It's some photos. I'll go ahead an' record this, okay?

BILL: Okay.

DETECTIVE: *(to tape recorder)* This is Monday, July twenty-two and I'm speaking with Bill Stojak concerning the murder of Susie Smith. *(to Bill)* We got a dental records match up, but...they want us to have personal identification of the body whenever possible, so...

BILL: You want me to identify...

DETECTIVE: Just a technicality. Procedure.

BILL: Okay.

DETECTIVE: Confirmation. We could ask somebody else...

BILL: Maybe that would be...

DETECTIVE: But they're all real shook up too.

BILL: You called 'em?

DETECTIVE: Yeah, they're pretty upset.

BILL: Guess it comes down to me then.

DETECTIVE: Appreciate your help. So I'll just lay these out.

He now reveals graphic and gruesome crime scene PHOTOS of the bloodied body of Susie Smith to Bill.

BILL: *(nauseous)* Oh, jesus christ shit! Oh fuck, fuck. Motherfucker.

DETECTIVE: If you recognize her...

BILL: It's...her. That's Susie.

DETECTIVE: 'Cause I've got color glossies in here if you can't positively...

BILL: NO! ... That's enough. It's her. ... Those fuckers, they musta been right inside her place.

DETECTIVE: We'll catch him. He'll get his, I guarantee it.

BILL: Susie was such a good girl. ... Why?

DETECTIVE: If I knew...

BILL: She was so sweet. Everybody liked her.

DETECTIVE: Lemme ask you some questions about that.

BILL: What? I mean didn't I already...

DETECTIVE: Who her enemies were.

BILL: I don't know. ... Nobody.

DETECTIVE: Think back on that night. You were out with... Who?

BILL: It was me an' Melissa...

DETECTIVE: Okay.

BILL: And Frank an' Susie. ... Oh, an' April dropped by our table, that's right.

DETECTIVE: Good. April. Anybody else?

BILL: No, that's it. There was other people, but not at our table. Nobody I recognized.

DETECTIVE: Okay, now last time we talked, you said Pete was there.

BILL: Pete, yeah. *(remembering, casually)* No, he's not there.

DETECTIVE: Alright, Pete's not there. So what happened?

BILL: We had some dinner, an' drinks, an' then Melissa an' Frank left...or might a been April left with Frank.

Detective flips through his note pad.

DETECTIVE: No, you told me...*(reads from pad)* "April goes back to other friends across room..."

The Detective feigns difficulty in reading the notes and shows it to Bill, who reads,

BILL: "...right after..."

DETECTIVE: "...right after band takes last break."

BILL: *(cautiously)* Yeah, that's right. *(beat)* Hey you got good notes. Can I see those?

Detective flips the notebook closed.

DETECTIVE: You guys had partied pretty hard?

BILL: Sure, it was a big day for us.

DETECTIVE: Oh, you didn't say...

BILL: We all got promotions at work.

DETECTIVE: Oh, so it's like a celebration? ... And Frank and Susie, they got along?

BILL: Totally cool.

DETECTIVE: No problems that night?

BILL: No that was Pete.

DETECTIVE: Well you said Pete wasn't there.

BILL: *(beat)* Oh, right. You're right.

DETECTIVE: So that leaves you and Susie.

BILL: Yeah, I guess.

DETECTIVE: So who had the argument with Susie? *(watching him)* See, last time you said Pete had this big argument with Susie outside right after closing.

BILL: Was that Pete? No, maybe it was...

DETECTIVE: Who? Frank and Melissa already left, an' Pete's not there. ... In fact, his alibi checks out...So the argument's about you driving her home?

Referring again to his note pad.

DETECTIVE: *(cont'd)* You said, "Susie asked me to drive her home."

BILL: *(flat)* Yeah.

DETECTIVE: 'Cause she'd been drinking too much, correct?

BILL: Yeah, she said that. Look, why are you askin' all these...

DETECTIVE: *(interrupting)* And you said, "Sure, I'll drive you," and you did that, right?

BILL: *(evasive, not hostile)* I already told you I drove off with her. Doorman'll vouch for that.

DETECTIVE: We talked to the doorman. I did.

BILL: Yeah?

DETECTIVE: He says you're arguing with Susie. Yelling at her.

BILL: Well, she didn't wanna go. She did but then she changed her mind.

DETECTIVE: *(overlapping)* I thought she asked you?

BILL: I told her she was too drunk to drive...

DETECTIVE: *(overlapping)* So you told her?

BILL: *(overlapping, quickly)* An' she wanted to. ... She's always had her eye on me. Susie digs what I got happening, you know...

DETECTIVE: She's dead, Bill

BILL: *(continuing)*...but she really gets off on me.

DETECTIVE: Bill, Susie's dead.

BILL: An' all she had to do was be nice.

DETECTIVE: Susie's dead! Her head's all crushed in.

BILL: *(explosive)* You think I wanted that?

DETECTIVE: I didn't say you wanted it.

BILL: I know, but you said...

DETECTIVE: Did you want her dead?

BILL: NO! She shoulda just come along that's all...

DETECTIVE: *(overlapping here)* But she didn't want to.

BILL: She likes me, I know it. I can tell. Everybody knows she wants me...

DETECTIVE: *(overlapping)* Is that why you did it?

BILL: So I BASHED her with my metal camera case... *(indicating his temple)* Right across here!

DETECTIVE: You're under arrest for murder.

Detective handcuffs him through the Miranda advisement. Bill gives no resistance and continues his diatribe. The following lengthy passages are spoken simultaneously.

DETECTIVE: *(cont'd)* You have the right to remain silent. Anything you say can and will be used against you in a Court of law. You have the right to be represented by an attorney and to have an attorney present during questioning. If you can't afford an attorney, one will be appointed by the Court to represent you. With these rights in mind, do you wish to speak with me without an attorney present?

BILL: I was so sicka hearing her crap. First she wants to go, then she doesn't, then half way home, she starts whining about her car's still back there. Well you LEFT it there you dumb bitch! I stop the truck, let her out. ... FAGGOT?! You call me a faggot, you fucking whore! So I pick up the case and I swung that motherfucker! But she wasn't even dead yet so then I... *(stoic, to Detective)* What?

DETECTIVE: *(cont'd)* Do you wish to speak with me without an attorney present?

BILL: About what?

DETECTIVE: You're under arrest.

BILL: Oh, okay.

DETECTIVE: Where'd you stash the case?

BILL: In a ditch. I covered it up with some leaves an' stuff.

DETECTIVE: Let's go find it.

Detective picks up his note pad and the recorder and leads Bill out the door in handcuffs.

BILL: Okay. ... I really do love her.

DETECTIVE: She's dead, Bill.

Consensual Sex

INSIDE A COURTROOM – *The witness, VALERIE SMITHSON, 23, is on the stand, having just given incriminating testimony on direct examination in the rape trial of defendant Gregory Morris, seated next to his counsel. The defense attorney, DAVID TALBOT, approaches for cross-examination in this felony jury trial. A Prosecutor and Judge are also present.*

TALBOT: Alright Miss Smithson, so you say my client Greg Morris forced sex with you against your will. Is that about it?

SMITHSON: Yes.

TALBOT: Did you have any bruising?

SMITHSON: The doctors examined me.

TALBOT: And found no evidence of forced sexual intercourse, isn't that correct?

SMITHSON: He didn't use force, he threatened. He told me... *(to the Judge)* Can I say this? ... He said was going to "fuck me."

TALBOT: That's all that was said?

SMITHSON: And he was holding me roughly. I told him to stop.

TALBOT: Did you tell him "no" when he said he was going to have sex with you?

SMITHSON: Yes, I said that.

TALBOT: One time.

SMITHSON: Once should have been enough, and I told him to stop.

TALBOT: Well, you told him to stop holding you roughly.

SMITHSON: That's right.

TALBOT: And when you asked him to stop holding you roughly, did he stop doing that Ms. Smithson?

SMITHSON: Yes.

TALBOT: So he'd been holding you passionately, firmly, but you wanted more tenderness so you asked him to hold you more gently?

SMITHSON: I didn't say that. You're putting words in my mouth.

TALBOT: Were you fully dressed at the time of this conversation, about sex?

SMITHSON: Yes.

TALBOT: Your blouse was unbuttoned, wasn't it?

SMITHSON: *(hesitant)* Yes.

TALBOT: And the lights were low, you both had glasses of white wine, and he'd kissed and caressed your breasts that night, all with your consent. Isn't that correct?

SMITHSON: *(defensively)* I am a respectable woman.

TALBOT: And my client is a respectable man. Now that's why you went out with him in the first place, isn't it true?

SMITHSON: I made a mistake. I should have trusted my instincts.

TALBOT: You like to rely on your instincts, don't you? Even if you can't put your finger on something, if you get that gut feeling...

SMITHSON: I have a very good sense of things, and my sense was that I was being raped.

TALBOT: You were afraid?

SMITHSON: Terribly afraid.

TALBOT: Well you have neighbors, don't you? Did you cry out for help?

SMITHSON: No.

TALBOT: But you did tell him "no". A simple "no" when everything else said "yes" – the wine, the kissing, the fondling...Did you think that he was a mind reader?

SMITHSON: No, it wasn't like that!! He forced me. I told him no. What else could I do?

TALBOT: Ms. Smithson, wait, now you already testified that there was no force used. Did you push him away? Get up off the couch?

SMITHSON: No.

TALBOT: *(changing tacts)* Ms. Smithson, how old are you?

SMITHSON: Twenty-three.

TALBOT: And up until that night, you were a virgin, weren't you.

SMITHSON: *(to the Judge)* Do I have to answer that? ... Yes.

TALBOT: And it embarrassed you to have sex, for the first time, with a man who you'd only dated a few times, didn't it?

SMITHSON: *(beat)* Yes.

TALBOT: Previously, you'd even...what? ... Told friends that you wouldn't have sex until you were married, hadn't you?

SMITHSON: How do you know...Yes.

TALBOT: So when you broke that vow. When you gave in to sexual feelings for Mr. Morris, you were sick with guilt, weren't you Miss Smithson?

She can't respond. She is overcome with regret. Talbot picks up subpoenaed telephone bills.

TALBOT: *(cont'd)* And after Mr. Morris left that night, you called your sister on the telephone and cried to her didn't you? ...(I have the telephone records).

SMITHSON: Yes.

TALBOT: You told her he'd forced you to have sex didn't you? ... Didn't you tell your sister that he'd physically forced you to have sex? *(pause)* She's on call as a subpoenaed witness Miss Smithson. If you'd like, we can...

SMITHSON: *(interrupting)* Yes. I told her he'd raped me.

TALBOT: Physically forced you.

SMITHSON: Yes, I said that to her.

TALBOT: But that was a lie wasn't it?! Mr. Morris had never used any physical force on you whatsoever, had he?

SMITHSON: No.

TALBOT: You lied to your sister that night.

SMITHSON: Yes.

TALBOT: But she called the police, and you told them the same story, didn't you?

SMITHSON: Yes.

TALBOT: Because you couldn't back down. You'd waited your entire adult life for this beautiful experience of sexual intercourse with a man you dreamed would be your husband. Then Mr. Morris came along, and he fucked you and left you alone! You told your own sister you'd been raped. The police showed up, and you couldn't back down could you?

SMITHSON: NO! ... No, I couldn't back down.

TALBOT: Well it's got to stop Miss Smithson. Look at my client and tell the truth. Look at the man you dragged into a criminal trial. You had consensual sex with Greg Morris, didn't you?

SMITHSON: I told him no.

TALBOT: But you relented, encouraged and consented to having sex with him. Isn't that what happened?

SMITHSON: I want this to stop! Judge please, make him stop.

TALBOT: It was consensual sex, wasn't it Miss Smithson? Miss Smithson! *(to the Judge)* Request the Court to direct the witness to answer! *(to the witness)* It was consensual sex wasn't it?! *(to the Judge)* Request that the witness be directed to answer!

SMITHSON: Yes, alright! I wanted to say no but I couldn't. I needed him. I wanted him. He was holding me. ... He told me things, softly, that he wanted me. ... I'm twenty-three years old! ... But it hurt, and then he left, and I felt so...violated...alone. ... It wasn't right. He should have stayed with me. He knew I needed him, but he left me. ... I never meant for this to happen. *(to Morris)* All I ever wanted was tenderness At least you could have given me that!

TALBOT: *(calmly, deliberately)* Your Honor. Motion to dismiss.

Couple, The

ON AN OCEAN BEACH AT NIGHT – *A couple, BOB, 40s-50s and SALLY, 20s, walks down the beach and sits on a sand berm overlooking the ocean. There's a full moon.*

BOB: The ocean air feels nice.

SALLY: Beautiful. Look at that moon.

BOB: It's made of green cheese.

SALLY: Why do they say it's green?

BOB: They don't want you to eat it.

He playfully takes a bite of her arm.

SALLY: *(laughs)* Am I a tasty treat?

BOB: Yes. *(pause)* Sally, remember the day the surf was up?

SALLY: Huge waves.

BOB: Pounding.

SALLY: Right out there.

BOB: It's peaceful now.

SALLY: Calm before the storm.

BOB: Right. I hope.

SALLY: You really love the ocean.

BOB: I really love you.

SALLY: Yes. I know. And I love you too.

BOB: Do you?

SALLY: Of course I do. You know that, right Bob?

BOB: I do, but it's good to hear it again. *(pause)* It's a funny thing, love. You make a commitment and you think it'll never end. And then, sometimes it does. What happens?

SALLY: Two people...growing apart.

BOB: Petty arguments. Something. Right?

SALLY: Think that'll ever happen to us?

BOB: No, not a chance.

SALLY: Why not? Why not us?

BOB: It just won't.

SALLY: We grow and change, don't we?

BOB: Not that way, no.

SALLY: Maybe we should. Some change is good. Right? So, maybe...

BOB: We should grow apart? I like the way we are. A couple, together.

SALLY: A couple.

BOB: Yes.

SALLY: Hmmm.

BOB: What does that mean? Hmmm?

SALLY: Nothing, don't worry about it.

BOB: I'm not worrying. Hey.

SALLY: Why do you say "hey"? There's something you don't like about me?

BOB: Hey, no. I mean, no. *(sincere)* I like everything about you.

SALLY: Okay, now that's not true. Everything?

BOB: You know what I mean.

SALLY: Do I?

BOB: Yes.

SALLY: *(slightly antagonistic)* Alright, then I know exactly what you mean. You like "everything" about me. No exceptions, no distinctions. Everything.

BOB: You're kidding, right?

SALLY: Not kidding.

BOB: Okay, point taken. Not everything.

SALLY: True?

BOB: *(hesitates)* Yes.

SALLY: You don't like everything about me.

BOB: No, I mean, yes, that's right. Not everything, only the best things.

SALLY: *(sweetly)* Really?

BOB: *(cuddling)* Yes.

SALLY: *(gently pulls away)* What, for instance, don't you like about me? My hair? My body? My intellect? The way I smile? My voice? The way we make love? What?

BOB: Let's not do this, honey.

SALLY: Honey, no, tell me – what don't you like about me?

BOB: *(looks at his watch)* Oh check it out, it's already late. We'd better get home. We'll have some hot chocolates.

SALLY: *(pseudo sincere)* Honestly, Bob, you can tell me. What little things don't you like about me?

BOB: Let's drop it.

SALLY: No, it's okay.

BOB: You won't hate me if I tell you?

SALLY: *(lying)* Of course not.

BOB: *(pause)* This is a trap, isn't it?

SALLY: *(lying again)* No trap. Simple question.

BOB: *(hesitates, evading)* Well what about you? Do you like everything about me?

SALLY: Yes. Everything. No exceptions. Now, back to my question.

BOB: You like the fact you think I don't like everything about you?

SALLY: It's not what I think, it's what you said.

BOB: And if I tell you, specifically, what I don't like about you, then you'll like that too, correct? ... Sally?

SALLY: *(evasive)* I wouldn't know that because it's something in the future. It hasn't happened yet. But, judging from past history, I'll still like everything about you, yes.

BOB: What past history are you talking about?

SALLY: Passed past.

BOB: Specifically, what?

SALLY: You saying you love me.

BOB: Oh.

SALLY: So you can do it. *(sweetly mimicking)* "What I don't like about you is..."

BOB: Baby, really, you've got this all wrong. Honey…

SALLY: *(coaxing, again)* "What I don't like about you is..."

BOB: Sweetheart...

SALLY: Come on, Bobby.

BOB: *(pause)* Oh I see, you're asking me a question.

SALLY: What?

BOB: A question. You're asking.

SALLY: Yeah.

BOB: So what do you mean?

SALLY: Do I mean?

BOB: Yes, what do you...

SALLY: Mean? I mean, what don't you like? About me?

BOB: About **you**. Well, I like everything about you.

SALLY: No. What don't you like?

BOB: *(lying, convincingly)* Nothing.

SALLY: That's not what you said.

BOB: It is, yes. About you, I like everything.

SALLY: You don't.

BOB: I **do**. No exceptions.

SALLY: No, that's what I said.

BOB: I just said that.

SALLY: You're saying exactly what I said.

BOB: I always said that.

SALLY: You didn't.

BOB: I did and I will.

SALLY: And you're lying.

BOB: I am not…

SALLY: *(interrupting)* Bob Richardson, you are lying to me.

BOB: I'm not, no. I'm simply clarifying an apparent and unfortunate misunderstanding, because the fact is, there's **nothing** I don't love about you. I love it all.

SALLY: I don't believe it.

BOB: Yes you do.

SALLY: *(unsure)* No, I don't, and now, you broke our trust by lying **and** you don't like things about me.

BOB: Sally, I've always said and I'll always believe that I love everything about you. You know that's the truth.

SALLY: It is? You have?

BOB: Of course, yes. Always.

SALLY: *(putty in his hands)* But a minute ago...

BOB: A minute ago never happened. Right now, I'm saying I love you and everything about you. No exceptions, all at once, in every way, every day, and that's it.

SALLY: Is that true? For real?

BOB: *(quietly, deliberately)* It is, yes.

SALLY: *(hugging him)* Oh, good. Me too.

She kisses him. After a moment,

BOB: Let's make hot chocolates at home.

SALLY: With marshmallows?

Bob nods.

SALLY: *(getting up)* You love me and I love you too.

BOB: In every way.

She kisses him. Then, as they leave, hand in hand...

SALLY: Are you sure though? 'Cause honestly, Bob, you can tell me. You can.

He doesn't respond. They walk off hand in hand.

False Witness

DURING THE DAY IN A RESIDENTIAL NEIGHBORHOOD – *a private investigator, TRENT FLEISCHLI, late-40s, knocks at the front door of a residence. An Hispanic woman, JULIA RAMIREZ, 40s, opens the door.*

TRENT: Good afternoon. Mrs. Ramirez? I'd like to speak with your daughter, Estelle.

JULIA: *(closing the door)* She's not feeling well today.

Trent produces his Private Investigator identification.

TRENT: I'm Trent Fleischli, a Private Investigator.

JULIA: Just the same...

TRENT: The attorney I work for represents Manuel Sanchez. ... He's charged with murder.

JULIA: She told the police everything she knows.

TRENT: This won't take much time.

Julia slowly opens the door to allow Trent to enter into,

THE INTERIOR OF THE RAMIREZ RESIDENCE – *where moments later, Julia leads ESTELLE, 17, into the living room. She does not appear to be sick in any way. Trent stands.*

TRENT: Estelle, I'm a Private Investigator. Trent Fleischli.

ESTELLE: *(defensive)* I told everything to the police.

TRENT: I understand.

ESTELLE: Plus, I'm sick today.

TRENT: You don't mind if I record this?

He produces a tape recorder from his jacket, and flips it on.

ESTELLE: I guess, yeah, but I shouldn't have to answer any more questions.

TRENT: *(to the recorder)* This is Trent Fleischli, March 23, 2006, interviewing Estelle Ramirez at 11:15 a.m. at her home in the presence and with the consent of her mother, Julia. Do each of you consent to this interview being tape recorded?

ESTELLE: Yeah.

JULIA: *(overlapping)* Yes.

TRENT: *(cont'd)* Okay, I just need to clear up a few things. I read the police report of your interview.

ESTELLE: Then you know that Manuel guy shot my friend.

TRENT: So the deceased, the kid that was shot...He was a friend of yours?

ESTELLE: Yeah, we all knew him.

TRENT: How did you know him?

ESTELLE: I don't know. Through school.

TRENT: Did he sell drugs?

ESTELLE: *(surprised)* Who told you that?

TRENT: Some other kids. Did you know he sold drugs at school?

ESTELLE: *(looks away, then...)* I don't know nothin' about that.

TRENT: But you did see Manuel shoot him.

ESTELLE: Yeah.

TRENT: Did you do anything to stop it?

ESTELLE: No...'cause I came around the corner just before.

TRENT: So, I don't understand, why were you going behind the building?

ESTELLE: What?

TRENT: Well, you said, you went around the corner just before he shot Rick. Why'd you go back there?

ESTELLE: *(evasive)* No, I heard a shot, then I ran over there. I was nearby.

TRENT: Okay, so you were at the corner of the building?

ESTELLE: *(pause)* No, not right there, but close.

TRENT: Let's back up. You heard a shot and went around a building to where it was fired?

ESTELLE: Three shots, yeah.

TRENT: That doesn't make sense to me. Nobody runs towards gunfire.

ESTELLE: Whatever.

TRENT: And your boyfriend, Steve Hernandez was there too?

ESTELLE: Who said anything about Stevie?

JULIA: *(overlapping)* Stevie was there?

TRENT: Somebody else saw him around, yeah. Did you talk to him?

ESTELLE: No. ... Yeah, maybe.

JULIA: *(to Estelle)* You never told me that, Estelle. You talked to Stevie? I told you never to talk to him anymore, ever.

TRENT: Stevie was back there with Rick?

ESTELLE: No.

TRENT: He was back there, I've got people who saw him.

ESTELLE: I don't know nothing.

TRENT: Stevie was there?

ESTELLE: I didn't say nothing to the police 'cause he has a bad rep, you know, from the drug selling thing, and I...

TRENT: Stevie sold drugs for Rick?

ESTELLE: No, the other way around.

TRENT: Rick worked for Stevie.

Estelle nods her head.

TRENT: *(cont'd)* Is that a "yes"?

ESTELLE: Yeah. Yes.

TRENT: Okay, so Stevie was back there with Rick.

ESTELLE: I don't know. I saw Stevie after Rick got shot. I saw Stevie first.

TRENT: Before you saw Manuel, you saw Stevie?

ESTELLE: Yeah, when he ran around the corner.

TRENT: Stevie?

ESTELLE: Yeah.

TRENT: Okay, so here it is: you heard the shots. Then Stevie ran around the building from where Rick was. Then you saw Manuel?

ESTELLE: You're confusing me.

JULIA: Estelle, did you see Manuel shoot Rick?!

ESTELLE: Okay, no. Not really.

TRENT: What did you see?

ESTELLE: Stevie said he'd kill me. I can't...

JULIA: Estelle Maria Consuello Ramirez, you tell this man the truth.

ESTELLE: Okay, okay. Stevie told me he saw Manuel shoot Rick.

TRENT: You heard shots, Stevie ran from behind the building. He tells you, what?

ESTELLE: That a wetback kid shot Rick…

TRENT: *(overlapping)* …which you didn't see.

ESTELLE: *(overlapping)* …and to forget I ever seen Stevie there or he'd kill me.

TRENT: *(cont'd)* Stevie threatened you?

ESTELLE: He was all, really losing it. Shaking.

TRENT: And you never saw Manuel shoot anybody?

ESTELLE: I didn't even know his name 'til the police told it to me later.

TRENT: And Manuel wasn't holding the gun?

ESTELLE: It was on the ground by Rick. Rick was dead.

TRENT: Manuel didn't run or say anything to you?

ESTELLE: I don't think he speaks English.

TRENT: Manuel never shot anybody.

ESTELLE: I didn't see the wetback do nothing. He was just standing a ways away. You know, like watching it go down.

TRENT: Then the police arrived?

ESTELLE: *(nodding)* Am I gonna get in trouble for all this?

TRENT: I don't know the answer to that.

JULIA: *(to Estelle, overlapping)* You are in big trouble with me.

Trent glances at his watch.

TRENT: *(to the recorder)* This interview's concluded at 11:22 a.m. *(shuts off recorder)* I'll see my way out. Oh, and Estelle, you better get to school today. You don't seem sick to me.

Trent exits.

Inner Voice

IN A LIVING ROOM AT NIGHT – *a GUY, 40s, reads a gripping book. A VOICE, ditzy/funky chatterbox female, early 20s, wanders in from nowhere in particular. They are never able to see each other.*

VOICE: Aren't you going to say hello?

Guy is startled, looking around. He thought he was alone.

GUY: Who's that?

VOICE: *(cheery)* Who else? It's me!

Guy is on full alert.

GUY: Where?

VOICE: Wherever you are.

Guy starts looking everywhere in the room to find this woman.

VOICE: *(cont'd)* Guess I broke the ice. Were you ever going to talk to me? *(sotto)* I thought it was kind of rude. *(pause)* Excuse me, what are you doing?

GUY: *(evasive)* Nothing in particular.

VOICE: You're breathing hard. I can always tell when you're breathing hard, which you seem to do a lot, I might add. *(slight smile)* And it's not always exercise if you know what I mean.

GUY: *(evasive)* I have no idea what you're talking about.

VOICE: *(mocking, in fun)* Oh, okay.

He can't find her anywhere.

VOICE: *(cont'd)* Are you hungry? I'm hungry.

Guy tries to compose himself.

GUY: No, yes, a little. Look, forget about food. ... This is a joke, right? Marty put you up to this?

VOICE: Who's Marty?

GUY: A buddy of mine. Can you see me?

VOICE: Not really, but I hear you.

GUY: News Flash, the girl I'm talking to actually hears me. ... I know, you're on the computer.

He grabs his laptop, peering into the screen. She makes a sound meaning "wrong answer".

VOICE: Baaaan! Not the laptop. *(taunting him)* If you promise not to tell...*(sing-song)* I'll-tell-you-a-secret.

GUY: What?

VOICE: Promise not to tell?

GUY: Yes.

VOICE: Good. *(confiding, whisper)* I think I'm inside you.

GUY: Yeah, well get out, there's no room.

VOICE: I'm serious. I'm inside your head.

Guy looks up as if to look inside his own head.

VOICE: *(cont'd)* It's frustrating being cooped up all the time. Nobody to talk to. I've got needs too. Ever think about that?

GUY: What the fuck. You know, I'm very NOT amused.

VOICE: It's no joke.

GUY: I'm calling the police.

VOICE: Go ahead. They'll think you're crazy, put you in a padded cell.

He picks up the phone and dials 9-1-1.

VOICE: *(cont'd)* Arrest you for me being inside your head. "Breaking and entry, Your Honor. It was an inside job." Lock you up, throw away the key.

GUY: It's ringing.

VOICE: "He was arrested for stalking himself! He wanted to plead Guilty, but she said, '**Not Guilty by Reason of Insanity!**'"

GUY: You think you're so funny? I'll show you funny.

VOICE: Maybe you're crazy. Did you consider that possibility? It's a proven fact, 12.3% of the populace experiences a form of psychosis.

GUY: I'm not crazy.

VOICE: *(singing)* Crazy, I'm crazy for living without you. Crazy for livin', crazy for tryin', crazy for loving you.

GUY: *(pleading)* Stop it, please.

He hangs up the phone, frustrated.

GUY: *(cont'd)* Fine, what am I thinking?

VOICE: That you're gonna kill Marty when you find him. Well, not *kill* kill him. But...

GUY: No, no, that's too easy. *(worried)* What am I thinking now?

VOICE: *(pause, worried)* That you're scared. Your cousin Bob was mentally ill, and you think it might be happening to you.

She's right. Guy freaks out.

GUY: Holy fuck. What the fuck is this shit? Stop it. Get outta my fucking head! Get out.

Holding his head, trying to keep the sounds inside.

GUY: *(cont'd)* You've been listening to what I do? How long have you been in there? What do you know? What should I know about what you know?

VOICE: Everything's okay. Chill a little.

GUY: How old are you?

VOICE: Early 20s?

GUY: And you're a woman?

VOICE: Let me check.

She looks at her boobs and kneads them with her fingers.

VOICE: *(cont'd) (upbeat)* I'm a woman, alright. But that doesn't mean you're a woman. You're a guy, I can tell that.

GUY: That's right.

VOICE: And how's that going? Being a guy.

GUY: *(not convinced)* Great, I guess. It's all good.

VOICE: And you don't like other guys or anything? ... Sexually.

GUY: *(defensive)* No! Fuck no. I'm all about liking pussy. Sweet pussy. Smooth, soft and juicy. Sometimes all I think about is getting laid.

VOICE: And how's that going?

GUY: As long as we have that clear.

VOICE: No prob.

GUY: But if I'm crazy, aren't the voices supposed to be irrational?

VOICE: This whole conversation's way out there. If somebody could hear you but not me, you'd be max'd out in the irrational department.

GUY: No.

VOICE: Big time.

She folds her arms and buttons her lip. We can't hear her but he still can.

GUY: Well, sure, once you know...I know I know you know now, but...I don't know if I knew you were...No, it's not like that, you're twisting...I am **not** being rude, you're the one...

He looks around, then thinks for a moment.

GUY*: (cont'd)* Okay, I get the point.

VOICE: Exactly. You sound a little wacko.

GUY: Oh.

VOICE: Over the edge.

GUY: Yeah.

VOICE: Flipped your wig. Zonko. A few cards short of a full deck. Crazy as a Lune...

GUY: I got the picture. Stop. *(laughs)* You know, it's nice, talking to you like this. After it's over, maybe you and I could meet. Have a Green Tea Frappuccino.

VOICE: Excuse me, I'm you. You'd be dating yourself.

GUY: *(realizing)* Holy shit, you're right.

VOICE: That's incest.

GUY: Right, yeah. So forget it.

VOICE: Look, we can make this work: you find girls you like, and I help you close the deal.

GUY: We team up?

VOICE: I know what chicks like, how they feel. You could do this.

GUY: I could?

VOICE: You'll be a happening guy.

GUY: Alright! You and me!

VOICE: There's limits: vacation days, paid sick leave, perks, but generally, yes.

GUY: Agreed, okay.

VOICE: You know, I like girls too.

GUY: You do? Really?

VOICE: Oh yeah.

GUY: Awesome. Okay, let's get started.

He grabs his jacket, and she leads the way out the door.

VOICE: Food first. What is it with you guys? Go all day, nothing to eat.

Janitor, The

DURING THE DAYTIME IN SAM ROSEN'S EXECUTIVE OFFICE — *A Man, "ED BILLINGS" is looking through documents on the desk of SAM ROSEN, who walks in reading a letter draft.*

ROSEN: *(surprised)* Can I help you?

BILLINGS: *(flashes a badge)* Ed Billings, CIA.

ROSEN: Central Intelligence Agency?

BILLINGS: That's right.

ROSEN: Of the United States?

BILLINGS: *(ignoring the question)* How well do you know your wife?

ROSEN: Sherry?

BILLINGS: We know her as 65803, aka "Sandra."

ROSEN: That's not her name.

BILLINGS: *(confidentially)* Your wife's a spy.

ROSEN: A **spy**?!

BILLINGS: **Eye**! A bug in my Eye. *(fingering his eye, blinking)* This is very confidential.

ROSEN: You're speaking about my wife?

BILLINGS: Yes.

ROSEN: She's a prep cook at Applebee's Diner.

BILLINGS: *(smiles)* So she fooled you too. Inside every Blue Plate Special is a state-of-the-art micro-dot cryptographic program.

ROSEN: I don't really see...

BILLINGS: Certain people would pay a lot for the keys to those cryptos.

ROSEN: In the Blue Plate Specials?

BILLINGS: That's right.

ROSEN: Then the kitchen work...

BILLINGS: *(interrupting)* A hoax, an elaborate hoax.

ROSEN: A hoax?

BILLINGS: Yes.

ROSEN: She never could cook a decent pot roast at home.

BILLINGS: She's not slinging hash at Applebee's.

ROSEN: She never goes to work...well she goes to work...

BILLINGS: Oh, she goes to work alright.

ROSEN: *(getting into it, laughing)* Does she ever. Living the spy life, laying low...

BILLINGS: Spy gadgets.

ROSEN: Danger, intrigue...

BILLINGS: Big money and scandalous affairs...

ROSEN: How big?

BILLINGS: We got a digital video. It's rather racy, but...

ROSEN: The money.

BILLINGS: *(smiling, nodding)* Oh, well...

ROSEN: *(smiling, nodding)* Well...

BILLINGS: Account numbers in the thirteen digits.

ROSEN: *(blurts out)* **Thirteen digits**!! *(softly)* Thirteen digits, oh my god. *(calculating, then)* Account numbers?

BILLINGS: *(flatly)* Yes.

ROSEN: What about the balances? How much? How big is big?

BILLINGS: The balances?

ROSEN: Yes.

BILLINGS: I'm not at liberty to confirm or deny balances.

ROSEN: *(pause)* Why are you here?

BILLINGS: National Security, Level Five priority. The duty load assigned to 65803 became so excessive as to possibly, very possibly, in all likelihood, almost certainly compromise her cover. Her life is in grave danger.

ROSEN: That's terrible.

BILLINGS: Yes it is. And reluctantly, we've decided to bring her out of the cold.

ROSEN: I've heard about that.

BILLINGS: No, you haven't.

ROSEN: *(correcting)* Except from you, right now.

BILLINGS: I'm not here.

ROSEN: Where are you?

BILLINGS: Anywhere but here. Think of me as...

ROSEN: *(quietly)*...elsewhere?

BILLINGS: You're sharp. Very sharp. A man of your stature, education. We're about to relocate Sandra to Antarctica... *(pacing, thinking, discovering)* Hmmm. ... Unless...and I'm thinking aloud here...No.

ROSEN: What? Unless what?

BILLINGS: Unless you two work as a team.

ROSEN: We're already married, it might work.

BILLINGS: Rosen...Can I call you Rosen? We may have stumbled onto something. You see, Sandra is deep cover, and if her cover's still viable...

ROSEN: *(quickly)* You could leave her in the cold!

BILLINGS: In place. We don't say "in the cold," only bringing someone "out of the cold."

ROSEN: Oh.

BILLINGS: Never the reverse. That's a dead giveaway.

ROSEN: Right.

Rosen nods.

BILLINGS: In place. Make a note.

Billings indicates to a pad on Rosen's desk.

ROSEN: *(he hurriedly does)* "In place."

BILLINGS: Now eat the note.

ROSEN: What?

BILLINGS: It's evidence. Eat it.

ROSEN: *(eating)* Oh, right.

BILLINGS: You could join her as a spy. Ferret intel, counter espionage probes...

ROSEN: *(starts to write)* Counter espionage probes...

BILLINGS: I wouldn't do that.

ROSEN: Oh.

Billings points to his mouth. Rosen eats the note.

ROSEN: *(cont'd) (mouth full)* And I do it right here at Office Depot H.Q.?

BILLINGS: No.

ROSEN: *(looks around, suspicious)* It's not really an office supply company, is it?

BILLINGS: I can neither confirm nor...

ROSEN: *(overlapping)* Nor deny. Of course.

BILLINGS: It's need to know. And what you need to know is that now...you quit this job and head to Applebee's.

ROSEN: Now?

BILLINGS: No exit interview. Out. And apply as...*(thinking)* A janitor!

ROSEN: *(exploring)* Not management? Golden parachute, executive package, car, perks...

BILLINGS: *(overlapping)* Too high profile.

ROSEN: *(digging)* Customer service? People-to-people supervision!

BILLINGS: *(overlapping)* Too low profile. ... But... *(reassuring)* You know how to push a broom, scrub floors, shine a toilet bowl?

ROSEN: *(flat)* Yes.

Shuttling Rosen toward the door.

BILLINGS: That's it then. You're a janitor at Applebee's. As time goes on, we'll be in touch with further instructions.

ROSEN: How much time?

BILLINGS: *(handing a notepad)* When the time comes, you'll know. Alright, write this out...

BILLINGS: *(cont'd)* I, Sam Rosen, being of sound mind and able body do hereby solemnly swear...

ROSEN: *(interrupting)* If I write, do I have to eat it?

BILLINGS: Yes.

ROSEN: Let's pretend I wrote it and pretend I ate it.

BILLINGS: Good, that's good. See, you got the hang of the spy business already. *(at the door)* Now, say nothing to your wife. Go directly to Applebee's and **become**...the Janitor. Become...the Janitor.

Rosen begins to speak.

BILLINGS: *(cont'd)* Ah ah! We'll be in touch.

Rosen walks out the office door. Billings gathers up the files he's interested in, sits at Rosen's desk with his feet up and punches in a number on his cell phone.

BILLINGS: *(cont'd)* Superior Office Supply? Joe? ... I've got the customer survey and product data files you wanted. Oh, and send one of your guys in for an interview. The Vice President of Marketing slot just opened up. ... You got it.

He smiles, hangs up the phone and walks out the door with the files.

Letter, The

LATE AT NIGHT IN POVERTY LAW CLINIC – *A Documentary filmmaker, GIL GANT, lenses an overworked attorney, DARLENE JOHNSON, 26, attractive. She's exhausted, paging through thousands of files and records.*

GIL: *(surgical)* Ms. Johnson, what happens at 10:00 a.m. if you're not able to find it?

DARLENE: *(flatly)* My client loses her house in a foreclosure sale.

GIL: And then what happens?

DARLENE: What?

GIL: If Miss Finch loses her house?

DARLENE: She's thrown out on the street. She has no place to live. She's retired with a very limited income.

He comes in closer with the handheld video.

DARLENE: *(cont'd)* I'm trying to concentrate here.

GIL: *(narrative voice)* It's three-seventeen a.m.. A letter lies hidden in tens of thousands of discovery documents received by Attorney Darlene Johnson only today at 4:55 p.m..

DARLENE: Four fifty-seven.

GIL: At four fifty-seven p.m.. And when your client tells you a key piece of evidence may exist somewhere in this veritable mountain of documents, what goes through your mind?

DARLENE: Putting you out of your misery goes through my mind, Gil. Please, stop the questions. There's thirty-some thousand pages before eight this morning – for a letter I need to stop the foreclosure.

GIL: And what does this letter say?

DARLENE: It's from the lender's attorney, advising my client of the deadline for saving her house.

GIL: For clearing the default by paying the loan.

DARLENE: Yes, except the date was wrong. It gave the wrong date and she relied on that. She's got refinancing now, but it's too late. The real date was last week and unless I can get a T.R.O., they're gonna sell her house – ten a.m. this morning.

GIL: *(directly to camera)* They're going to sell the poor lady's house.

DARLENE: There's too many papers, and they counted on that producing all this stuff at four fifty-seven – knowing I couldn't finish, knowing I probably wouldn't find the letter in time. And unless I get lucky...

GIL: *(interrupting)* Here, let me move.

DARLENE: What?

He changes camera positions.

GIL: Do that part again. You "probably wouldn't find" it.

DARLENE: *(indignant)* Are you putting me on?! *(composing herself)* Knowing I probably wouldn't find the letter in time. And unless I get lucky, I won't find it, and her house gets sold.

GIL: And Ms. Johnson, how does that make you feel?

DARLENE: *(puts down the papers)* It makes me feel like you don't give a shit!

GIL: Wait a minute, I give a... I care.

DARLENE: Are you getting all this now? 'Cause it's real life, not a story. It's happening right now!

GIL: It's raw justice. *(to camera)* You're watching, Raw Naked Justice.

DARLENE: But you're not a part of it.

GIL: I'm a part of it.

DARLENE: Filming. Watching it happen.

GIL: That's what I do.

DARLENE: It's what you do. *(getting up)* Gil, would you stand by while terrorists set a bomb?

GIL: No, I wouldn't.

DARLENE: *(gaining momentum)* Would you watch a swimmer drown?

GIL: I'd throw him a line.

DARLENE: Run over baby chicks?

GIL: Absolutely not!

DARLENE: Let Miss Finch lose her house?

GIL: Never!

DARLENE: *(flatly)* Good, then look for the letter.

GIL: I have to keep a professional distance.

DARLENE: Gil, I need help. If two of us go through this stuff, we got a shot.

GIL: You're the attorney, not me.

DARLENE: I'm the attorney, right. I'm overworked and underpaid. A grocery clerk spends more time with customers than I can spend with mine. And I get six boxes of discovery the night before a foreclosure sale. Well it's just wrong, but you're putting it all on tape. So good for you.

GIL: *(continuing to videotape)* What are you saying?

DARLENE: *(breaks down)* That I'm hungry. And tired. And my client probably deserves a better lawyer. And there's not enough time. Maybe Judge Harris was right, I got my "head in the clouds." What's the use?

GIL: You'll be okay.

DARLENE: No, the clinic was a bad idea. I shoulda done criminal defense with my dad.

GIL: You needed to go your own way. He wanted that for you. Right?

DARLENE: Yeah.

GIL: There aren't many lawyers for the little people – to stand up for their rights. They're out on a limb and nobody wants to crawl out with 'em. The limb gets narrow, branches sticking out everywhere – poking, scratching. Every inch and it sags way down. *(animated)* Will it bend or will it break? And if breaks, do you go down with it? Hundreds of feet, falling, plummeting towards mother-earth at break-neck speed. Look out 'cause here it comes, the Killer Fall!

DARLENE: *(stoic)* Is this supposed to cheer me up?

GIL: Huh? *(calming down)* Well, for you, it won't break, it just bends. And you're on that limb, and you help a lot of people who couldn't otherwise get representation. You gotta do the number, get down with the plan, hang with the big dogs...

DARLENE: *(overlapping)* Let me put it in more practical terms: If I don't find that letter, she's gonna sue me for malpractice.

GIL: Oh.

DARLENE: And this poverty law clinic ends up a coin laundromat. So, excuse me while I "get down" with the impossible task.

She goes back to looking through the documents, hunting for the letter.

GIL: *(pause, softly)* Maybe I could do something?

DARLENE: *(ignoring him)* Another close-up? It's okay.

GIL: We could call someone.

DARLENE: My secretary's out of town. There's nobody to call.

GIL: What if I help?

She looks up.

DARLENE: You're filming. You never stop filming. You're Gil...

GIL: *(deflated)*...Gant, Documentary Filmmaker, Two Golden Tripod Awards.

DARLENE: Three.

GIL: Three, right.

He sets down the camera and takes a stack of documents.

GIL: *(cont'd)* I could look through some of this. It's a letter from a lawyer, right?

DARLENE: You're not breaking some documentary filmmaker's Code – Rule 26A-dash-two?

GIL: Probably, but Rule 26B-dash-one overrides.

DARLENE: What's it say?

GIL: *(slight smile)* It says for me to get off my ass and help, or words to that effect.

DARLENE: You know, Gil, after your film is done, there's one other rule I want you to break.

GIL: What's that?

She kisses him.

GIL: *(cont'd)* Why did you do that?

DARLENE: You'll find out later.

GIL: *(he likes her too)* Let's find the letter, then finish this film.

They dig into the documents.

Municipal Complaint Department

MUNICIPAL COMPLAINT DEPARTMENT

DURING THE DAY AT THE MUNICIPAL COMPLAINT DEPARTMENT – *a CLERK wears a Smiley Face button which says, "Have a nice day." He stands at a booth which bears a sign, "Municipal Complaint Department." A female customer is leaving. Number 67 pops up on the Take-A-Number device.*

CLERK: *(to the departing customer)* If you don't like the water, ma'am, get outta the kitchen! *(looks at the Take A Number device)* Next complaint! Number 67.

A Persian MAN walks up, handing the Clerk his complaint written on a slip of paper. As the Clerk is reading.

MAN: They will not permit me to serve jury duty.

CLERK: Nobody wants jury duty. What's your problem?

MAN: Are you talking to me?

CLERK: What?

MAN: Are you talking to me?

CLERK: You asked about jury duty.

MAN: To serve my country.

CLERK: What country's your country?

MAN: Don't get smart.

CLERK: Are you a citizen?

MAN: Of course I am a citizen.

CLERK: *(pause)* …of the United States?

MAN: That's a very personal question. Are you analyzing me? Do you think I need help?

CLERK: This is a help desk, yeah. For complaints.

MAN: And I've got complaints. A lot of complaints. I can't sleep. I have aches and pains. My skin itches. I am a nervous wreck. Analyze that.

CLERK: We don't take that kind of complaint.

MAN: And I won't take it either. … I got to do my duty and serve a jury.

CLERK: Serve on a jury.

MAN: What?

CLERK: You want to serve on a jury.

MAN: Yes, exactly. *(leans in)* Do you think Maury tells his wife everything? I want you to bring him to the game tonight.

CLERK: What game? Who's Maury?

MAN: I been telling you your whole life: Don't talk on the fucking phone! Right? Now you understand.

CLERK: About the jury?

MAN: Are you being smart with me? 'Cause I don't think you wanna be a smart mouth.

CLERK: I'm trying to help you.

MAN: *(continuing)* The last guy who was smart with me isn't feeling so good right now, if you catch my meaning.

CLERK: He got a cold?

MAN: No.

CLERK: Fever?

MAN: No.

CLERK: Irritable bowel?

MAN: No!

CLERK: Aches, pains, depression, nightmares?

MAN: No, that's me. Say, you wouldn't happen to know a good shrink?

CLERK: I don't. Look, what's your name? I can't make it out on this form.

MAN: DeNiro.

CLERK: *(writing it out)* DeNiro. First name?

MAN: Bob.

CLERK: *(flat)* Bob DeNiro?

MAN: That's right. Bob, Bobbie, Robert. Are you stupid or what? Did you hear what I said? Don't buy anything. Don't get anything. Nothing big. Didn't you hear what I said? What's a matter with you?

CLERK: You're not Robert De Niro. You're Indian, Pakistani, Arab...What are you?

MAN: *(stares, then)* I am Persian.

CLERK: Oh.

MAN: You remember the guy I told you about? Wasn't feeling so good?

CLERK: Yeah.

MAN: *(serious)* He swims with the fishes.

CLERK: You mean...?

MAN: Yeah.

CLERK: Oh.

MAN: That's right.

CLERK: *(realizing)* He's a snorkeler. Fishes, swims...

The Man stares the Clerk down, then breaks into a laugh.

MAN: You almost got me! That's funny.

CLERK: *(puzzled)* Yeah, well...

MUNICIPAL COMPLAINT DEPARTMENT

The Man laughs long and too loud, as De Niro did in the movie theater in Cape Fear.

MAN: *(cont'd) (serious)* Now, help me procure jury duty.

CLERK: You gotta be registered to vote.

MAN: Voting, okay, sign me up too.

CLERK: No, you gotta be a citizen of the U.S..

MAN: A citizen?

CLERK: Yes.

MAN: ...of the United States?

CLERK: That's what I've been tryin' to tell you. Right.

MAN: *(pause)* Well that's a stupid rule. What happen to "jury of your peers"? They can arrest you, charge you with crime without you being a citizen. This is discriminatory.

CLERK: Are you charged with a crime?

MAN: *(leans in)* I remember Jimmy Macalwayne on the yard. Used to say, "You wanna be makin' moves on the street, you have no attachments. Allow nothing to be in your life that you cannot walk out on in 30 seconds flat if you spot the heat around the corner". You remember that?

CLERK: I think...

MAN: *(interrupting)* I do what I do best. I take scores.

CLERK: (*proud he got it*) **Heat.** I liked that one.

MAN: Thank you.

CLERK: (*confiding*) You think you might get pinched?

MAN: Pinched? I am never goin' back. Never.

The Man walks off.

CLERK: What about the **jury**?

MAN: Thirty seconds flat.

CLERK: (*calling out*) Gimme something from Midnight Run! That was a good one. Midnight Run! (*to the waiting area*) Okay. ... Next complaint! Number 68.

MUNICIPAL COMPLAINT DEPARTMENT

No Money

IN AN URBAN AREA DURING THE DAY – *Two men, JIMMY and DOYLE sit on a bench, mindlessly preoccupied. Jimmy is a schemer, Doyle a dreamer. Doyle is fooling with his jacket zipper, while Jimmy tries to open a combination padlock without knowing the combination. Both are very hungry, both down on their luck, and Jimmy has about had it with Doyle's lame ideas.*

DOYLE: Why do you figure they start the zipper at the bottom? You ever think about that? 'Cause you know, if it started at the top, you could like, leave the bottom open, and have the top closed.

JIMMY: Yeah, but what about the top?

DOYLE: What?

JIMMY: Ya want the top open, and the bottom closed, you're fucked, is why.

DOYLE: Okay, I see what you mean.

JIMMY: Besides numb nuts, nobody wants the top closed and the bottom open.

DOYLE: I don't know...

JIMMY: Look, 'stead of thinkin' about zippers, think of a way to get us some food why don't you.

DOYLE: What I'd do for a Big Mac. I am gettin' real hungry.

JIMMY: Come on Doyle. Big Mac doesn't even compare to a Double Cheese burger with fries. Cheese oozing down, sticky fingers, french fries soakin' in catsup, gotta lick it off.

DOYLE: Stop it Jimmy, my stomach hurts I'm so hungry.

JIMMY: We gotta eat. It's goin' on two days now.

DOYLE: Okay, well we got options here.

JIMMY: What kinda options? We got no money.

DOYLE: We could sell those flower deals. You know, the pushy people – sell 'em at the off ramps.

JIMMY: And where do we get the flowers to sell genius? Wonder if we just go out an' plant the seeds first. Grow the flowers?

DOYLE: Where do they get 'em?

JIMMY: They **buy** the flowers Doyle, 'cause they already got money. See they got money to start with. We got zip.

DOYLE: Oh.

JIMMY: So the flower idea, that ain't happening.

DOYLE: We could always ask people for some money. I'd give myself money if I had a sign hangin' over my head.

Jimmy bops Doyle with Jimmy's hat.

JIMMY: Oh now there's a real bright idea. Gonna make us into beggars. That's rich Doyle, livin' on hand-outs.

DOYLE: *(serious)* Jail food's pretty good. Remember that meat loaf they had, an' those green beans? They was kinda stringy but...

JIMMY: I ain't goin' back to jail Doyle.

DOYLE: Jimmy, I had some food, but you ate it. You ate my cookie.

JIMMY: And last week I shared my can of tuna with you Doyle, if you'll recall.

DOYLE: I found that can.

JIMMY: Yeah, but I opened it. Remember? I had the can-fucking-opener.

DOYLE: It was my last cookie Jimmy, an' I'm getting' real hungry. You ate my last cookie.

JIMMY: So now you gonna harp about a chocolate chip cookie.

DOYLE: Oatmeal! It was a oatmeal cookie.

JIMMY: So what? Is that a federal crime? If you'd a been hungry you'd have eaten it. I was hungry so I ate it.

DOYLE: I was hungry.

JIMMY: You know what? I'm sick of this shit! Doyle, do we have the god given right to eat? You and me.

DOYLE: Yeah.

JIMMY: It's a free country, am I right? Is this a free country? Bill of Fucking Rights. It says right there, a guy's got a right to life and liberty, am I right?

DOYLE: Yeah?

JIMMY: We don't eat, we're gonna die.

DOYLE: Yeah!

JIMMY: That's right. No food, no Life. **They gotta let us eat!**

DOYLE: Bill of Rights! ... Life, liberty and the pursuers of happiness.

JIMMY: It's illegal for us not to be able to eat. We got protections. Our forefathers and shit wrote that. Against the law for them not to let us eat.

DOYLE: So...what? Police could walk in, arrest the McDonald's workers for not lettin' us eat?

JIMMY: Arrest the whole god damned lot of 'em. What we oughta do, is just go in there, take the food, just like that.

DOYLE: *(serious)* Walk right in, take the food?

JIMMY: Oh yeah.

DOYLE: We could do that?

JIMMY: Sure we could. We're hungry. We walk in, we take it out.

DOYLE: *(laughing)* Like Chinese take out.

JIMMY: Food to go. Chalk it up to Liberty. Ha!

DOYLE: Bring a flag in with us!

JIMMY: That's it! Embassaries of the hungry and the weak... and the "disenfrenchfried"!

DOYLE: That's great Jimmy, that's so great! We wouldn't even need money. Whenever we was hungry, we'd just go in an' take the food.

JIMMY: *(pause)* Yeah well that's the problem. Can't just go back in there every time we need more food.

DOYLE: Oh yeah?

JIMMY: We'd be goin' in every day.

DOYLE: Yeah.

JIMMY: Twice a day. ... We need real money.

DOYLE: I guess you're right.

JIMMY: So...we rob a liquor store, or a bank. Get some money.

DOYLE: Whatever we rob, it better be right near a McDonald's. Like in the same shopping center. And we'd better do it soon.

JIMMY: Can't be the same shopping center, Doyle. "'Scuse me, but I'm gonna rob you, and by the way, see that McDonald's over there?"

DOYLE: See what you mean.

JIMMY: Call the cops on our asses. We're in the McDonald's line. Fucking cops drive through the take-out, get this call, robbery in the same fuckin' shopping center. There we'd be.

DOYLE: *(smiling)* Us just standin' there, holdin' the money we stole.

JIMMY: So that's it. We rob a liquor store, then go buy food someplace else.

DOYLE: But I think we better get the food first, buy it or whatever. 'Cause we can't do a robbery this hungry.

Jimmy knocks on Doyle's head.

JIMMY: Hello, anybody home? Hello? Think about it. We get the money, from the robbery, to buy the food. Robbery then food.

DOYLE: But that ain't so smart Jimmy. I can tell you're real hungry, 'cause you ain't thinkin' straight. We go in on a robbery thing, clerk throws out a curve, maybe asks you a question. Your name, or where you live or somethin'. You ain't gonna be thinkin' so quick on your feet, 'cause you're so friggin' brain dead.

JIMMY: They ain't gonna be askin' no questions.

DOYLE: What if they do? Think about it. It's a possibility Jimmy, a real possibility.

Jimmy repeatedly hits him with the hat.

JIMMY: They won't got no questions Doyle!

DOYLE: Maybe we buy the food on credit. McDonald's maybe loan us the money.

JIMMY: There won't be no "credit".

DOYLE: *(long beat)* Hey Jimmy, you know what?

JIMMY: What?

DOYLE: *(excited)* I got some money on me.

JIMMY: What are you sayin'?

DOYLE: I just remembered! Twenty bucks. I had twenty bucks when we got arrested. They put it in the little plastic baggie, the kind that turns red when you zip it closed?

He digs into his back pocket

DOYLE: *(cont'd)* There it is, cash money! We can eat! I forgot I had it.

Jimmy snatches the money in the plastic baggie.

JIMMY: Unbelievable. C'mon, let's get some food. *(walking off)* Just unbelievable.

Doyle follows close behind.

Not Guilty

INSIDE A COURTROOM IN SESSION – *where persons in the Courtroom quietly shift in their seats, waiting for the proceedings to recommence. The Judge has yet to arrive, and the defendant, WILLIAM TAGGERT, male, 50s-60s, listens to whispers from his attorney, JASON PARKER, a weathered man in his 50s. Both Taggert and Parker wear suits and ties, although defendant Taggert's suit is borrowed and is slightly off style and size.*

JOEL SCHULTZ, male, 50s, sits at the opposing counsel table, reviewing a neat stack of documents, and arranging his note pad and pen for easy access. Schultz is a seasoned and hardened prosecutor in this criminal trial which is about to conclude.

A Court Reporter records the proceedings stenographically. Also in the Courtroom is a uniformed BAILIFF and an empanelled JURY of twelve men and women.
An inner door of the Courtroom opens, and JUDGE Preston J. Wilkins, 50s, male, graces the Courtroom with his presence.

BAILIFF: Be seated and come to order. This Court is now in session, Honorable Preston J. Wilkins, Judge presiding.

The Judge takes his seat at the Bench and the clamor of the Courtroom quickly expires to a chilling silence.

JUDGE: Alright, we're back, on People versus William Taggert. Ladies and gentlemen of the jury, this morning we heard closing argument by the prosecution. Please remember the Court's admonition to refrain from forming any judgment in this case until jury deliberations. *(turning to Parker)* Mr. Parker, it's time for your closing argument to the jury on behalf of your client, Mr. Taggert.

Attorney Parker rises at the counsel table. He appears to be well prepared and eager to present his case.

PARKER: Yes, thank you Your Honor.

Parker makes eye contact with certain jurors, and steps smoothly over to behind his client, Mr. Taggert, touching his shoulder. Bordering on a rehearsed preamble to an argument, Mr. Parker proceeds.

PARKER: *(cont'd)* The prosecution has argued for a Guilty verdict against Mr. Taggert, on charges of First Degree Murder of the young girl in the parking lot. But there's a reasonable doubt in this case. Mr. Taggert is an innocent man, falsely accused, and it's your duty to find him Not Guilty.

Parker smiles briefly and moves back to his end of the counsel table. He picks up his somewhat disorganized stack of notes, files and reports. He steps to a podium a few feet further away from his client. There's a moment of awkward silence.

PARKER: *(cont'd)* Now, there was eyewitness testimony in this case, where Miss Sherman identified the defendant.

FLASHBACK – COURTROOM – *MISS SHERMAN, 23, attractive, not wearing glasses, preens for the jury. Parker is fumbling with his briefcase lock at the time of this critical testimony and doesn't notice as she glances down at something in front of her on the witness stand.*

PARKER: *(V.O.)* There were problems with the I.D.. It wasn't solid. I just didn't think she was positive.

MISS SHERMAN: *(overly dramatic)* He's the one, I'm absolutely positive. There's no mistaking that face.

The jury looks over at the defendant. Miss Sherman is staring defiantly at Mr. Taggert now.

PARKER: *(V.O.)* But that's only the beginning...That is, it's your job to determine her credibility.

BACK TO SCENE INSIDE THE COURTROOM – *where Parker pulls out a corner of a document from a folder.*

PARKER: The fact is, eyewitness identification is unreliable, and believe me, the books are filled with cases of mistaken identifications involving look-alikes.

He extracts a NEWSPAPER ARTICLE on mistaken identification involving people who are highly similar in facial appearance. Schultz stands immediately.

SCHULTZ: Objection, your Honor! That document's not in evidence, and there's no evidence in this case whatsoever about any look-alikes.

JUDGE: Sustained. Mr. Parker, you know better. The jury's to disregard Mr. Parker's reference to look-alikes. Continue please.

Parker sorts the document back into its folder.

PARKER: Alright, well, in this case...

Parker pours himself a small paper cup of water at the counsel table. It's flimsy and too small for any normal drink of water. But Parker regains some composure as he fumbles for the police report.

PARKER: *(cont'd)* The police themselves weren't sure Taggert did it. I mean, right? That's right. Remember, after the arrest, they brought him directly to Sherman's house for the I.D..

FLASHBACK – OUTSIDE SHERMAN'S HOUSE AT NIGHT – *Two UNIFORMED POLICEMAN haul Taggert out of a marked police car and walk him up to Sherman's house, alone, in handcuffs, in a manner highly suggestive of guilt. He wears a dark blue sweatshirt, jeans and tennis shoes. Sherman is outside on her porch, puts on her glasses and peers at Taggert.*

PARKER: *(V.O.)* In handcuffs, alone.

MISS SHERMAN: *(to the police officers)* He's the one? *(pause)* Yeah, okay, he's the one. It's him.

PARKER: *(V.O.)* So that's it, because the police weren't sure either.

BACK TO SCENE INSIDE THE COURTROOM – *where Parker has a vague notion that he's touched on something, but he doesn't know what.*

PARKER: And that initial identification of Mr. Taggert wasn't in court, and it's hearsay, so what good was it? It was the identification right here in Court that...Well, so that's two identifications of the defendant.

Parker wipes sweat from the back of his neck.

FLASHBACK – COURTROOM – *as a police BOOKING PHOTO of Taggert, marked Evidence Exhibit #23, sits in front of Miss Sherman on the witness stand. In the booking photo of his head and shoulders, Taggert wears a dark blue sweatshirt from the night of his arrest.*

FLASHBACK – COURTROOM – *where Ms. Sherman looks down at the photo and then over to the defendant and points confidently to Taggert.*

BACK TO SCENE INSIDE THE COURTROOM – *as Parker is visibly worried, searching for words and lacking in confidence in his own argument to the jury.*

PARKER: But it's the in-Court identification that's, well...The importance of the...So you should simply disregard the other one. *(moving on)* Now, I know Miss Sherman claimed she had a clear view and was certain, but she had a...ah, there was a... hesitation. You may have noticed it. I know I did.

Parker's gaining steam now.

PARKER: *(cont'd)* She wouldn't look me in the eye. In fact, she couldn't take her eyes off Mr. Tag...Well, a hesitation, and...

FLASHBACK – AN OUTDOOR PARKING LOT AT NIGHT – *In a DIMLY LIT parking lot, WE SEE a KILLER, mid-40s, wearing jeans and a dark blue jacket, pull a GUN on a YOUNG GIRL, 17, any ethnicity. The Killer is definitely not Mr. Taggert.*

PARKER: *(V.O.)* She's only one witness to a violent crime and ...I mean, how could she possibly know who...actually see the man?

Suddenly, the Killer SHOOTS the Young Girl. Miss Sherman, across two lanes of cars in the parking lot, is startled by the shot and fumbles with her eye glasses in her purse. The Killer grabs the Young Girl's purse. Miss Sherman finally puts her glasses on and looks in the direction of the shot. By this time, however, the Killer has turned his back and is fleeing the scene. Miss Sherman basically sees a man dressed in dark blue fleeing the scene with the Young Girl's purse in hand.

BACK TO SCENE INSIDE THE COURTROOM – *Parker himself seems to be actually puzzling over whether Miss Sherman could have seen the man. It's as if he's thinking aloud now, quietly, without censorship of his own thoughts.*

PARKER: We don't even know the lighting was that night. ... It might have been dark out there. How dark? The testimony? It was a parking lot...

Pulling out of his internal digression, as if making a new discovery.

PARKER: *(cont'd)* What was the lighting like out there? The prosecutor didn't ask that question! ... And the witness didn't bring it up. So how do we know? I mean, she might have said the lighting was dim, for example.

For the first time, Parker himself recognizes that this may have been important testimony in the trial.

PARKER: *(cont'd)* I suppose we could have viewed the site. Your Honor, perhaps the evidence could be reopened on this issue...

The Judge almost imperceptibly shakes his head in the negative.

SCHULTZ: Objection, there's no motion pending.

JUDGE: Sustained.

PARKER: I...No. So, we just don't know. Well that's it then. How can you believe Miss Sherman if you just don't know?

The jury is dumbfounded at Parker's obvious incompetence. Parker takes another "drink" from the now empty and somewhat crumpled tiny paper cup, and loosens his tie.

PARKER: *(cont'd)* And Mr. Trigger...*(corrects himself)* **Taggert**, didn't do it. That's the important part now. ...The defendant, Mr. Taggert, is a family man. He has a family. Wife and two daughters.

FLASHBACK – INSIDE TAGGERT'S LIVING ROOM – *a neat but very sparsely furnished living room at the home of a man who is barely paying his bills, but making it. Taggert is sitting with his WIFE, mid 30s, attractive but timid, watching TV. He wears jeans, a dark blue sweatshirt and tennis shoes. Their two daughters, KRISTI, 4 and JULIE, 7 years old, walk into the room.*

KRISTI: *(jumping on his lap)* Hi daddy.

JULIE: Mommy, have you seen my doll with all the red hair?

WIFE: No, honey.

TAGGERT: I saw it. What do I get if I find it for you?

JULIE: A big kiss!

TAGGERT: Okay. It's in the car, wait right there.

Julie is excited to find her favorite doll again. Taggert hands Kristi off to his Wife, gets up and walks out the front door, closing it behind him.

OUTSIDE TAGGERT'S HOME – *Taggert walks to his car in the driveway just as a black and white patrol car cruises by. The Two Uniformed Officers spot Taggert wearing clothing similar to the robbery/killing report, stop the patrol vehicle and order Taggert to the ground.*

OFFICER #1: *(gun trained on Taggert)* On the ground, now. Keep those hands where I can see them.

Taggert complies. The front door opens slightly as Taggert's Wife and children look out.

BACK TO SCENE – INSIDE THE COURTROOM –
Parker continues his rambling appeal to sympathy.

PARKER: What would they do without him? They care for the man. Not everyone has that support.

Parker drifts off in the caverns of his own desperate thoughts.

PARKER: *(cont'd)* I guess he's lucky in that sense. His family stayed with him in his time of need. *(recovering)* What was I...ah, oh, so...his family. ... He's not a wealthy man. He can't go out an' hire the finest lawyer in town. ... He's got a good lawyer, I don't mean to say that. I mean to say...What I mean is, I ah, I did my job. And he's innocent. How can anyone be that sure of the killer's face? It's ridiculous, right? Because the sound of the gunshot must have distracted her. She testi... Would have said that...If I'd asked her about that, I'm sure... *(forces it out)*...she would have said that.

SCHULTZ: Objection, assumes facts not in evidence.

JUDGE: *(routinely)* Sustained. The jury will disregard.

PARKER: Alright. The shot. She was asked that, in a round about...Yes! Indirectly she was asked about the shot. She said she heard it when she was looking right at Mr. Taggert! ... I mean the kill...at the killer. No, no wait a minute.

FLASHBACK – AN OUTDOOR PARKING LOT – *where again, from another angle, WE SEE the robbery go down. A SHOT is fired. It startles Miss Sherman. She fumbles for her glasses, but by the time she puts them on and looks over at the Killer, he has already grabbed the Young Girl's purse and is running away.*

BACK TO SCENE – INSIDE THE COURTROOM – *as Parker wipes sweat off his face that's been building up.*

PARKER: That she looked him in the eyes and...No, did she? *(picking up his notes)* Let me...What did she say?

With hands noticeably shaking, hopelessly plowing through his jumbled notes of testimony, police reports and...he pulls out an INVOICE for an unpaid law office utility bill, marked "60 DAYS PAST DUE."

PARKER: What's this? Oh.

He puts it down.

PARKER: *(cont'd)* It's awfully hot.

He wipes his brow with a handkerchief. He steps to the counsel table pouring himself another tiny cup of water. Defendant Taggert is worried now and gulps down a few cups of the water. Parker returns to the podium.

PARKER: *(cont'd)* She looked like a drinker to me!

Schultz rockets to his feet, aggressively.

SCHULTZ: This is outrageous, your Honor. Objection. There is nothing...

PARKER: *(interrupting)* Alright, alright. I know it's not part of the evidence, but believe me Your Honor, I know a drinker when I see one.

The Judge RATTLES the Courtroom with a heavy slap of the gavel on the Bench.

SCHULTZ: Objection to this entire line of argument! There is no testimony whatsoever about Miss Sherman being a drinker, consuming alcohol, drugs or anything else whatsoever under the sun that could possibly impair her.

JUDGE: Sustained! Sustained! Mr. Parker, you're warned. You are that close to being in contempt of this Court.

PARKER: I have no contempt for this Court.

JUDGE: Well this Court has contempt for you. Now, the jury shall completely disregard Mr. Parker's comments about the witness drinking. Which she wasn't. In fact, the jury is instructed that the witness was not drinking alcohol, nor consuming drugs of any kind, nor was she impaired in her judgment in any manner at the time or in the aftermath of the criminal act. There.

FLASHBACK – THE OUTDOOR PARKING LOT – *at Miss Sherman's car, Miss Sherman is waiting on her cell phone for 911 to answer. She takes a slug from a whisky flask.*

MISS SHERMAN: *(to her cell phone)* There's been a shooting. ... Parking lot at the corner of...Oh I don't know. It's around Anaheim Street and Obispo. ... A man dressed in dark clothes. He ran off with the woman's purse. ... Okay, I'll stay on the line.

She takes another slug to calm her nerves.

BACK TO SCENE – INSIDE THE COURTROOM –
Schultz is happy with the Court's instruction to the jury.

SCHULTZ: *(smiles)* Thank you, Your Honor.

Schultz sits down again.

JUDGE: Mr. Parker, approach the Bench, at sidebar.

Parker and Schultz approach the "sidebar" at the side of the Bench. The Judge leans over.

JUDGE: *(cont'd) (with quiet intensity, to Parker)* Mister, I don't know what your problem is, but you'd better snap out of it or they'll be some serious consequences with a capital-god-damned S.C.

Schultz discreetly bare-kuckle-greets the Judge.

SCHULTZ: *(softly)* U.S.C.

The Judge smiles slightly, then turns his attention back to Parker.

JUDGE: Is that clear, counsel?

Parker nods sheepishly and he and Schultz return to their counsel table positions.

JUDGE: *(cont'd)* Continue, Mr. Parker.

Parker takes hold of the podium as if to keep himself from slowly slumping.

PARKER: Alright, yes, thank you Your Honor. So. ... So... distracted by the shot. I'm sure she heard the shot. Yes, of course she did. But she couldn't have seen, ah, remembered the killer's face. That's right. People have a hard time remembering what they ate for breakfast, where they put their keys again, or, or where we had our last drink...*(wiping brow)* And well, Miss Sherman was unreliable. She has to be, because Mr. Taggert's innocent. Can't you see that?

FLASHBACK – INSIDE THE COURTROOM – *as Ms. Sherman smiles at the Judge in an overly familiar manner.*

PARKER: *(V.O.)* It's true, she was calm up there testifying. But so what?

JUDGE: Thank you so much Miss Parker, you're excused now.

Ms. Sherman gets up, straightens her short skirt, nods to the jury and steps out of the witness chair. She catches the eye of one of the male jurors and smiles slightly. He smiles slightly.

PARKER: *(V.O.)* That doesn't mean you should believe her.

BACK TO SCENE – INSIDE THE COURTROOM – *Parker is losing it.*

PARKER: I could be calm, and that wouldn't mean you should...

There's a twitch to a side of his face. It's slight, but we've just noticed it.

PARKER: *(cont'd)* See, there must be an explanation. That's why we're here, for me to show you that. I want to do that, and I would have, you know, brought in his alibi witness if there was time.

SCHULTZ: Objection, Your Honor, he's doing it again. There is no evidence. There is no evidence of any alibi witness. I am dumbfounded, Your Honor. It's outrageous.

PARKER: Yes, but the case, it came up to trial so fast! How did it come up so god-damned-fast?

JUDGE: *(exasperated)* **That's it!** Mr. Parker, this Court finds you in contempt of court for the use of that profanity, and for your alluding to alibi testimony that doesn't exist. *(to the jury)* Ladies and gentlemen of the jury, you are ordered to disregard any reference to alibi witnesses, and in that regard, the Court instructs you to find that there was no alibi witness. *(turning to Parker)* Now Mr. Parker, we're going to get through this closing argument one way or the other, and again, I want to impress upon you the seriousness of your misconduct here and the consequences.

PARKER: *(to the jury)* Alright. Well, my apologies to the jury and Court. So...his wife. Now, she wasn't a defendant, of course, but the defendant, Mr. Taggert here, referred to her in testimony and...No. Is that right? And I would have brought her in, you know, if, but...But that testimony wasn't necessary. The jury instruction! Testimony of the defendant alone can raise a reasonable doubt! So, in that sense, an alibi witness, his wife and children...isn't absolutely nec...essary. I planned on using her. I even served a subpoena. Did I?

Shaken, questioning his own memory, Parker gropes through his papers endlessly, hands shaking, face twitching, sweating.
PARKER: *(cont'd)* I'm sure I...

Parker looks at his client, then back to the jury, as if they themselves might hand him the missing document, the crucial witness, that elusive bit of testimony. Somehow, Parker feels betrayed by the jury itself.

PARKER: *(cont'd) (to the jury)* Look, I can see what you're thinking. I've been here before, and I know that look. *(angrily)* You can't wait to vote GUILTY, can you?! Jump to conclusions and assume the worst. Just like my wife when she found the bottle in my brief case. Well that wasn't it! ... And, and it isn't her problem. IT'S MINE! So **don't you look at me like**...

Parker catches himself. The entire Courtroom is stunned into silence by Parker's verbal rampage. Slowly, deliberately and desperately Parker continues.

PARKER: *(cont'd) (desperate)* Ladies and gentlemen, you don't want to make a mistake here. This is an innocent man. *(almost begging)* Wait, okay, look, he hasn't had every break in life but he's had a productive life. He's not a broken man like m...He's a decent man.

A silence shrouds the Courtroom while Parker aimlessly pages for the Nth time through his disheveled papers. Then Parker shatters the silence.

PARKER: *(cont'd)* Maybe I didn't do the best possible job. Don't you think I know that?! *(into his stack of paper)* Gotta go back. Investigate this case again. Send out a subpoena. I have some questions I didn't...*(to the Judge)* Your Honor. Wouldn't this be the kind of case where...Perhaps the prosecutor...

Schultz shows not even the slightest sign of complicity.

PARKER: *(cont'd)* The prosecu...well, Mr. Schultz, could reopen this file and...*(stripped bare)* Alright, maybe I'm NOT the attorney I should be, I don't need you to tell me that. No one's asking for your opinion, anyway. But this shouldn't be happening to Mr. Taggert! Please...NO! This man is INNOCENT!

The Bailiff is on his feet at this last outburst. Shell-shocked, Parker stares blankly at the jury. The Judge breaks the bubble.

JUDGE: *(sarcastic)* Parker, anything further, on behalf of your client?

PARKER: *(stoically)* What? ... No. That's all.

JUDGE: Rebuttal, Mr. Schultz?

SCHULTZ: *(sarcastically)* That won't be necessary your Honor.

The Judge turns solemnly to the jury.

JUDGE: Alright then. Ladies and gentlemen of the jury. You've heard the evidence, jury instructions and now...argument of counsel. Select a jury foreperson, discuss the case, and let us know when you've arrived at a verdict.

FADE TO BLACK – THEN, INSIDE THE COURTROOM HOURS LATER – *as the jury finishes filing into the jury box and sits down. The defendant and the two attorneys are standing. In the back row of the jury box, the jury FOREPERSON, female, has a card in her hand.*

JUDGE: I understand you have a verdict. Could the Foreperson of the jury please rise?

The Foreperson rises from her seat.

FOREPERSON: Here your Honor. I'm it. We all selected me!

JUDGE: *(smiles)* Fine. Ms. Foreperson, kindly read the jury's verdict.

Taggert whispers a question to Parker, who becomes distracted trying to quietly answer his client.

FOREPERSON: We, the jury in the above-entitled cause do hereby find the defendant, Jason Parker, guilty of Murder in the First Degree.

JUDGE: The record shall so reflect.

The Bailiff retrieves the jury verdict card from the Foreperson, and hands it to the Court Clerk, who files it in the official court case file.

PARKER: Excuse me your Honor, what was that? I'm sorry. Who?

FOREPERSON: We find Mr. Parker guilty, your Honor.

PARKER: What?!

JUDGE: *(to the jury)* Is that your verdict?

The jury unanimously nods in the affirmative, and Taggert begins to "routinely" collect his file papers on the counsel table and place them into what used to be Parker's briefcase.

JUDGE: *(cont'd)* The jury is congratulated on its service here. Without your efforts, justice could not be served. This jury is discharged. Thank you.

PARKER: What is this?

JUDGE: *(to the Bailiff)* Mr. Bailiff, place that man in custody, immediately.

The Judge points directly to Mr. Parker. The Bailiff swiftly spins Mr. Parker and handcuffs him. The jurors collect their personal belongings and begin to file out of the jury box.

JUDGE: *(cont'd)* Put the defendant back into lock-up. Bail on appeal's denied.

PARKER: *(to the Bailiff)* Take your hands...

Bailiff roughly "escorts" Parker from the Courtroom.

BAILIFF: Let's go. Move it!

As Parker is taken out of the Courtroom...

PARKER: Wait a minute. STOP!

A calm resumes as Taggert is finishing closing "his" briefcase with the trial notes and documents. Taggert consults his calendar.

TAGGERT: August 12 for the sentencing date, Your Honor?

JUDGE: That'll be just fine, Mr. Taggert. It's always a pleasure.

TAGGERT: Thank you Your Honor, I feel the same.

JUDGE: *(nodding to Schultz)* Mr. Schultz.

SCHULTZ: *(acknowledging the Judge)* Your Honor.

The Courtroom empties. The Judge to his chambers, and Taggert and Schultz through the Courtroom doors to the Hallway, joined by the jurors. On the way out the doors,

FOREPERSON: *(to Taggert)* We had to vote guilty, Mr. Taggert. It was such a crime.

Only the water jug and a few crumpled cups remain on the counsel table. After a few beats, a JANITOR, 50s, male, black, wrinkled and definitely blue collar, walks into the Courtroom with his broom. As he is sweeping the room and tidying up, the Janitor addresses the audience.

JANITOR: I understand defendant Taggert was charged with murder. Now that's a serious charge, yes it is. And he was innocent all right, free of any guilt. Family man...Tried by a jury of his peers. One of those all-American type juries. *(raises his eyebrows)* You gotta figure that with all this fancy woodwork, the books and school smarts an' all, well the man woulda been proved innocent. And he should've been, but nobody counted on that Parker fella. *(laughs)* No, it's hard to count on him, that's a fact...The man was a lawyer for sure, and this wasn't a first case. No no, he'd, he'd lost quite a few over the years. Had kind of a knack for it. That's right, you might say he specialized in losin' cases. If these walls could talk. Well they don't have to, 'cause everybody else does. People say he'd get lost in his work. I just think he got lost, period. He didn't mean nothin' by it. Suppose he had his own problems. 'Course, that didn't much help his clientele. And he kept comin' back. Very sad. Sad to see it happen, over and over. But Parker, he lost his last case this time! Caught up in the **Wheels of Justice**. Took a wrong turn. Spun out. Wiped out. Somethin'. So that's it, gotta go. Keepin' the place tidy. That's my job, and let me say this about that—I take pride in my work.

Janitor tosses the paper cups in the trash can, wipes down the counsel table with a rag from his pocket and walks out the back door with his broom.

FADE TO BLACK.

Passing Through

INSIDE A CAFÉ – *on an afternoon in a cozy little town in Northern Arizona. A handsome man, CRAIG, late-40s, who believes that anything in life is possible, walks in. He wears a business suit.*

KATIE, early 20s, a young woman with a world of hope in her eyes, is cleaning a glass. She walks over to him. He's sweating. That's the first thing she notices when she gets close. The sweat on his forehead.

KATIE: Terrible hot out there today.

CRAIG: I'm tellin' you.

He doesn't notice her yet, or look up. He fumbles with a newspaper, and a set of reading glasses, which he puts on.

KATIE: Can I get something to cool you off?

CRAIG: *(without looking up)* Maybe a swimming pool with a big-old diving board.

He looks up, finally, from the mess he's created in opening up the newspaper on the table, and sees her. He smiles, then, self-conscious about the glasses, takes them off.

CRAIG: *(cont'd)* Sorry.

KATIE: You look good in glasses. Are you a teacher or something?

He pockets his glasses.

CRAIG: *(disappointed)* Not really, no.

KATIE: Where'd you drive from?

CRAIG: Phoenix. You get down there?

KATIE: I don't have a car. I had one once. Tony Billings fixed me up with a lime green Ford.

CRAIG: I like Fords.

KATIE: A '64 Fairlaine. Posi-traction, four on the floor, slick tires and a souped up 427. She'd top-out at a hundred twenty-eight.

CRAIG: Pretty fast.

KATIE: Ramsey clocked me once out on the Interstate. He's the town Sheriff.

CRAIG: Oh yeah?

KATIE: That's right. So, where was I?

CRAIG: Something cool to drink.

KATIE: *(catching herself)* Oh, sorry. It's been a while since I thought about the Ford Fairlaine.

He wipes his brow again. Then he ambles over to the counter.

CRAIG: It's okay, take a break. I'll just pour me a glass of ice water.

She sits down across from him at the table, and relaxes, putting her feet up on a chair. Absentmindedly, she flips off her shoes and brushes back her hair.

CRAIG: *(cont'd)* Would you like one?

KATIE: Don't mind if I do. Thanks. So you're from Phoenix?

CRAIG: Winslow, actually. It's north, a little east of...

KATIE: *(interrupting)* Cornville's small but I know where Winslow is.

He brings them over, hands her one and sits down.

CRAIG: Toast. ... We're in Cornville?

KATIE: Better believe it.

CRAIG: It's a funny name.

KATIE: What's wrong with Cornville?

CRAIG: Nothing, I suppose. Cornville, Arizona, sounds okay. But how 'bout Cornville, Massachusetts.

KATIE: Or, Cornville, New Jersey.

They laugh. He really notices her now.

CRAIG: I'll bet you're the prettiest little thing in this town.

KATIE: I won the Miss Cornville Rodeo crown when I was fourteen.

CRAIG: Is that right? ... My name's Craig. Craig Pendergrass.

She laughs.

KATIE: From a long line of Pendergrasses?

CRAIG: Very long. And what's yours?

KATIE: Katie Hooper. ... From a long line of Hoopers.

CRAIG: *(overlapping)*...of Hoopers.

They smile. She takes a sip of her ice water, never taking her eyes off him. It's a quiet connection between them.

CRAIG: *(cont'd)* You think I could get a sandwich to go? I got a pretty long drive.

Katie's back into her waitress mode, her bubble burst.

KATIE: Oh, sure.

CRAIG: I don't mean to trouble you.

She goes behind the counter and starts to make up one of her specialties.

KATIE: It's okay. *(she regroups)* I'll make up one a my specialties.

CRAIG: Actually, if...

KATIE: *(continuing)* It's got two layers of bologna, one layer of pressed turkey meat, and two kinds of cheese, American and Swiss. I call it my "International" sandwich.

CRAIG: Throw some mayonnaise on there. I don't like it too dry.

KATIE: I knew you'd like mayonnaise. There's all these health freaks out there, don't know how to eat anymore. 'Fraid a little mayonnaise's gonna give 'em heart stroke or something.

CRAIG: It's all white an' pasty. Maybe they think they'll get all white and pasty too.

KATIE: Get that tired look in their eyes.

CRAIG: One bite, just keel over. Epitaph says, "Here lies Fred. Ate some mayonnaise...now he's dead."

KATIE: (overlapping)...now he's dead."

They laugh. She's finished making and wrapping up the sandwich and walks it over to him.

KATIE: *(cont'd)* Three dollars.

He pays for the sandwich.

CRAIG: Well, thanks.

KATIE: If you need some lunch again...

CRAIG: *(overlapping)* When I drive to Phoenix again...

They stop, smile and indicate to the other.

CRAIG: *(cont'd)* I'll be down this way next week. Maybe I could stop in.

KATIE: *(smiles)* Or call me and I could deliver some food to go.

CRAIG: *(smiles)* Good idea.

KATIE: *(continuing)* I lived in Cornville all my life, but I got ideas on other places too you know.

CRAIG: *(beat)* I'm gonna be goin' now.

He turns to leave, then comes back, picking up his sandwich.

CRAIG: *(cont'd)* Forgot this.

Then he hands her a card.

CRAIG: *(cont'd)* Here's my card. Just so you know I'll be back.

KATIE: I don't have a card.

CRAIG: *(awkwardly, he shakes her hand)* Nice meeting you. Real nice.

KATIE: Me too.

CRAIG: Bye.

KATIE: *(quickly)* Could I ask you a personal question?

CRAIG: Okay.

KATIE: You're not married or anything are you? I don't mean to pry or nothin', but...

CRAIG: *(overlapping)* Me? No. Years ago, yeah, but no. No wife, no kids. ... And you?

KATIE: Single. No kids yet. Okay. Bye, Mister...*(looks at the card)* **Pendergrass**.

He leaves. She looks at the card again.

KATIE: *(cont'd) (sotto)* Katie Hooper Pendergrass.

She smiles, sits down and tucks the card away for safekeeping.

Prisoners

EXT. MIDDLE EAST TOWN – COMMERCIAL BUILDING – ESTABLISHING SHOT – DAY

A bleak, war-torn commercial zone. Bombs explode nearby and gunfire is heard in the distance.

INT. CELLBLOCK – CONTINUOUS

A stark, sixty-four square feet cold concrete box, with a high ceiling. One light dangles from a short cord.

Curled in a ball, in one corner, is JULIE, early 20s, lost, tormented and alone. Sweat soaked hair is all that is visible of her head as she quietly weeps. Her wrists and ankles show heavy bruising.

From time to time WE HEAR the powerful but muted rumblings of bombs exploding nearby.

INT. INTERIOR HALLWAY – CONTINUOUS

GUARD #1 and GUARD #2 drag an American soldier down the concrete hallway towards a massive steel door. They insert a key, open the door and...

INT. CELLBLOCK – CONTINUOUS

Toss Lieutenant Commander ALAN "AJ" JENKINS, 24, inside. AJ wears only a pair of Airman's pants. He has been beaten badly, particularly to his face. He's convulsively in pain but alive.

The Guards slam the door shut. After a moment, Julie peers through her twisted and matted hair. She's beautiful.

JULIE: *(to AJ)* Are you...[okay]?

Her voice dies out before the end of the thought. Is her accent Midwestern United States? AJ doesn't respond.

JULIE: *(cont'd)* Are you...an American?

After a few moments, AJ moves, pulling himself together and sitting up, in pain. His ribs are broken, face beaten.

AJ: Who are you?

Only silence in response.

AJ: *(cont'd)* How long...

They're interrupted by a LOUD POUNDING *on the door.*

GUARD #1 *(O.C.) (heavy Serbian accent)* Quiet! No talking!

Moments later, WE HEAR footsteps of Guard #1 walking away.

AJ: I'm Lieutenant Commander Alan Jenkins, but they call me AJ.

He moves slightly toward her. Outside, a bomb SCREAMS IN, detonating nearby, shaking the building. The light flickers.

JULIE: Two days.

AJ: What?

JULIE: *(faintly)* They got us two days ago. Supply convoy. In the outskirts.

AJ: You holding up?

She begins to quietly weep.

AJ: *(cont'd)* You'll be okay.

JULIE: *(a beat)* I know.

AJ scans the room for the first time. A concrete box with no ventilation, no holes except under the door, and no toilet. Filthy. Sweating, he moves to the door and looks under it, to the hallway.

JULIE: *(cont'd) (shivering)* I'm so cold.

EXT. HALLWAY – CONTINUOUS

It's empty.

INT. CELLBLOCK – CONTINUOUS

AJ tries to stand, grimacing in pain. His right ribs and shoulder are bruised badly.

JULIE: Did they do that?

AJ: No. On ejection I caught the framing, a strap, something. I was screaming at 10,000 feet. No one could hear.

JULIE: You'll be alright.

AJ: Could use a cold beer.

They laugh, quietly, and AJ winces in pain, making them laugh even more. AJ moves closer to Julie. He reaches to touch her, quiet her, but she pulls away sharply. He backs off.

AJ: *(cont'd)* What's your name?

JULIE: Julie.

AJ: Julie. *(a beat)* I almost got away.

JULIE: How?

AJ: A river near my drop point. Got in an' drifted.

JULIE: How did...

AJ: *(interrupting)* Went inta shock, came to shore. They saw me.

JULIE: Wait, don't...

He looks over. Fear, shame and painful memories begin to sweep over her.

JULIE: *(cont'd)* Don't tell me any...*(begins to sob uncontrollably)*...anything. They burned me, tied me. They... raped me. Over and over. I feel so...dirty.

She curls up.

AJ: I'm here. It's okay.

He reaches out for her again. She swings at him, hitting his shoulder. He jerks back. She lashes out instinctively.

JULIE: No! That's what they want. They'll make me talk! They want you to tell me things. Stay away! Stay...away.

Slowly, he touches her hand. Slowly she takes his hand. It's Beauty and the Beast.

AJ: Julie, it's okay. I'm right here.

JULIE: *(shaking, deliberate)* Don't tell me anything.

AJ: No, well, I wasn't...

JULIE: Promise. Even where you're from, or the river, or... I know why they put you here and... They'll do it again, for what...you say. Don't.

AJ: I won't. Nothing. I promise.

Heavy FOOT STEPS shuttle towards them, down the hallway outside. A key rattles. The door swings open. Guard #1 and Guard #2 storm in. AJ resists but is knocked aside.

GUARD #1: *(slapping Julie brutally)* I told you **quiet**!

He grabs her by the feet and drags her out through the doorway, followed by Guard #2. The door slams closed and locks. AJ dives for the door and watches as they drag Julie spread eagle down the cold cavernous hallway.

AJ: You god damn perverts! *(sotto)* Leave her alone.

FADE TO BLACK.

FADE IN:

INT. CELLBLOCK – LATER

A key rattles. The door opens. AJ is alone in the back of the room. An INTERROGATOR, 48, tall, neatly groomed, a sophisticated look, deeply muscled and intense dark eyes, steps inside. He locks eyes with AJ, seated across the room, licks his forefinger slowly, smiles and leaves the room.

FADE TO BLACK.

FADE IN:

INT. CELLBLOCK – LATER

The door opens again and Julie is deposited in the room by the two Guards. Blood stains are now openly visible in the crotch of her military pants. In a daze, weak and stoic, she lies there, motionless. The door closes and, O.C., the Guards WALK AWAY down the hallway.

AJ goes to her, lifts her up and lays her on the bench. Kneeling beside her, he strokes the matted hair from her face. Slowly, her hands move to her face, wiping, wiping with increasing intensity.

JULIE: Get it off, off me! Get it off!

AJ starts wiping her face, then licks his hand and wipes her face. She tenses, but slowly relaxes and places her arms between her legs. Quiet.

JULIE: *(cont'd)* Why are they doing this? I don't know anything. Don't tell me.

AJ: *(gently)* I won't.

JULIE: Thank you...

AJ: *(interrupting)* I...

JULIE: ...for holding me. *(pitifully)* What Am I doing here?

AJ: *(calming)* Be quiet now.

JULIE: *(tenderly)* I was in school.

AJ: What?

JULIE: Before.

AJ: Oh.

JULIE: I enlisted. Well, I got pregnant, then enlisted.

AJ: You're pregnant?

JULIE: No. My boyfriend, he didn't want...He didn't...

AJ: Oh.

JULIE: So, I...

AJ: It's okay. Be quiet. You'll get home. You'll see.

JULIE: I felt bad when I did that, to my baby. I...So I joined, after the abortion. And he left me.

AJ: Be quiet now.

JULIE: I'm afraid. Don't let them hurt me again, please AJ.

She clutches to his arm with both hands, pulling him into her closely. The steam from their faces now mixes in a macabre air dance.

AJ: *(firmly)* Be quiet.

FADE TO BLACK.

FADE IN:

INT. CELLBLOCK – LATER

The two are asleep in each others' arms, seated on the floor in the corner of the room. The door SLAMS open, waking and startling them. Interrogator walks in with Guard #1 and Guard #2. A look of terror fills her eyes.

Rushing up, Guard #2 rips them apart from each other and immobilizes AJ on the ground. Guard #1 holds Julie firmly by the hair.

Interrogator speaks English with only a slight Serbian accent.

INTERROGATOR: This girl has plenty of miles on her, but she'll go days before hemorrhaging causes death. *(introspectively)* Some say sex is more exciting that way.

AJ struggles against Guard #2's hold. No chance.

AJ: You scum sucking freak. She's a woman!

INTERROGATOR: I know that in the most personal way. But really, I'm very bored.

AJ: She doesn't know anything. She's infantry, for christ's sake.

INTERROGATOR: Oh, we know that too.

AJ: What do you want from her then?

Interrogator begins to laugh heartily.

INTERROGATOR: Absolutely nothing. It's what we want from **you** my friend, Mr. Airman.

He extracts a pair of WIRE CUTTERS from his pocket. AJ's eyes are big as saucers, and struggles to free himself again. No luck.

INTERROGATOR: *(cont'd)* We can't very well kill you. Not if we want the target and acquisition tactical positioning data. So, we will take the woman apart, little by little instead. Worst case, we have some fun on the way.

AJ: You sick pig.

INTERROGATOR: Music to my ears. You call me the pig. Yet, Americans bomb our cities, terrorize our people. I have a daughter of my own, you know.

AJ: Save it.

INTERROGATOR: And then, sending girls to do a man's job.

Julie grabs Guard #1's hand grasping her hair and slams her fist into his kidney, breaking free of his hold on her. She runs to AJ, striking Guard #2 in the head, before she is tackled by Guard #1.

JULIE: AJ, Help me! Oh, god, help!

AJ: *(struggling)* Leave her alone!

While Interrogator holds Julie with an armbar, both Guards hold and hit AJ severely to the stomach. They then take the girl and start out the door, leaving AJ gasping for breath on the floor.

INTERROGATOR: *(holding the wire cutters)* Between screams, we listen for your call. Let me know when you want to talk.

The Guards begin to haul the kicking and screaming Julie out the door. Her cries are muffled by the thick meat of Guard #2's hand. Desperately, AJ catches his breath, frozen in his stare at the unfolding horror.

AJ: **Let her live!**

AJ reaches frantically for the top BUTTON of his trousers, rips it off and jams it between his teeth. They all freeze in surprise. He bites down hard, then almost immediately, his head falls forward and he collapses, dead. Cyanide poisoning. Slowly, the Guards release Julie, who stands in shock.

INTERROGATOR: Damn.

Interrogator goes to AJ and finds a piece of the button. He examines and smells it.

INTERROGATOR: *(cont'd)* Cyanide.

Julie now speaks in a distinct Serbian accent. Straightening herself,

JULIE: You stupid fools. How could you let that happen? Didn't you search him?

INTERROGATOR: Yes, but the button...We didn't know about the button. I took...

JULIE: *(interrupting)* Shut up and get him out of here.

The two Guards drag AJ out of the room, as Julie watches in disgust. Interrogator starts out of the cell then stops, turns to Julie and acknowledges her superior rank with a snap salute.

FADE TO BLACK.

FADE IN:

INT. CELLBLOCK – LATER

Where the door opens and it's another American PILOT, early 20s, beat up, a rag-doll.

He's thrown onto the floor by Guard #1. The door SLAMS behind him. Pilot wears only dark gray sweat pants.

On the bench, WE SEE Julie, curled up and shaking like a battered child.

FADE TO BLACK.

Private Eye

LOS ANGELES – 1958, IN A 2ND STORY OFFICE.
A gumshoe meets with his latest bombshell client.

PRIVATE EYE: So what is it about your thing? Maybe it's I heard it fifty other times from fifty other dames with the same tired, teary eyed innocence. Maybe I been burned one too many times. You know?

These dames, they look like a million bucks, but never have a dime for their next cup of coffee. I mean, what is it with beautiful broads these days? It's like they look for the worst low-life crumbs that crawl outta the shadows, then expect sympathy when it suddenly turns sour.

I'm tellin' ya, if you were my kid sister, I'd ship you back to the Mid-West and be done with it. And that's that.

Your story, this one, I can't figure. Maybe I'm just another sap fallin' for a smooth line from a silky lady, but I got a hunch with you. I figure you're at the end of your rope and your story's straight.

Or maybe you got an angle, but I'll tell you this: if your Sweeny's just another bum, with no heat, who dropped you for the little lady at home, then I'll make you the loser, and you can put that in the bank.

So here's the deal. I'm expensive, but the best and get results. Three twenty-five a day plus expenses; a grand by next week. I protect you and lean on Sweeny to lay off, and you raise the grand. Simple.

Private Eye moves toward the office door.

PRIVATE EYE: Alright, let's go. Tonight, you stay at my place. I'll take the couch; we're old friends. Now, tell me again, this time with all the particulars: when did you first notice this louse following you?

Prowler, The

THE LIVING ROOM OF AN UPSCALE HOUSE – *a young woman, JEANNIE, mid to late 20s, attractive but worn down from years of recreational drug use, prowls through the furnishings of a home, searching for something. She's sweating and desperate.*

JEANNIE: It's here. I know it's god damned here.

Eventually, she finds an expensive NECKLACE hidden behind some books. She pockets it.

JEANNIE: *(cont'd)* Got it, you fuckers.

There's a noise of footsteps approaching the front door, then of keys in the lock. Jeannie hurriedly replaces the books to the shelf, moves away from the bookshelf and faces the door. A MAN walks in, mid to late 40s, upper middle class.

JEANNIE: *(cont'd)* Oh good, you're here. Somebody broke in, did all this.

The Man looks around, stunned.

MAN: Are you okay?

JEANNIE: Yeah, I'm cool, thanks. What are you doing home?

MAN: I forgot a patient's file. It's a complicated case and I... Why aren't you at the clinic?

JEANNIE: Oh, 'cause you know, I was with my sponsor, but then he had to leave and I wanted to get some sweaters and stuff, but I forgot to ask him for a ride and by that time he was gone...Well I asked, but I'm not sure he heard me, and so I caught a ride and they dropped me off and stuff and I was gonna call you for a ride back, but you know, it was like this when I got here.

He walks around, picking up some things, thinking about what she had told him.

MAN: Did you check the rest of the house?

JEANNIE: There's nobody here.

MAN: So you checked?

JEANNIE: *(beat)* No, 'cause I just got here, but there's nobody...I didn't hear anybody.

MAN: Is anything missing?

JEANNIE: I don't think so, I probably surprised him and they went out the back or something.

He looks at the outside door lock again.

MAN: You came in this way?

She nods.

MAN: *(cont'd)* The door lock's not tampered with.

He looks toward the back and then walks out of the room momentarily.

MAN: *(O.S.) (cont'd)* Nothing's been touched back here. ... The back door...

JEANNIE: The dead bolt?

He returns to the living room.

MAN: Still locked. We better call the police.

JEANNIE: No, no one's here. Maybe you can give me a ride back to the program after I get my sweaters and stuff, 'cause I probably shouldn't be out too long. And can I borrow some money, please?

MAN: They don't want that there. You can't have cash, 'cause then people start buying drugs and that's what the clinic's all about: no drugs. So, no, I can't give you money, but if I don't reach your sponsor, I'll give you a ride.

JEANNIE: No, I'll be okay.

He's starting to doubt his daughter's story, but is still giving her the benefit of the doubt.

MAN: Get your sweaters and things and I'll give Dave a call. I've got a new patient right after lunch.

JEANNIE: *(overlapping)* No, Dave's not around, I mean, his cell phone's off. I already tried calling him.

MAN: You called Dave? When?

JEANNIE: Just before you got here, I was gonna ask him for a ride home.

MAN: *(incredulous)* You called your sponsor?

JEANNIE: Yeah, 'cause you know, when you weren't here...

MAN: So you called him after you got here and saw all this? To ask for a ride?

JEANNIE: *(beat)* No, before.

MAN: I thought you said you were gonna call me?

JEANNIE: I don't know, I called him. His phone's off. You're confusing me.

MAN: *(beat)* Did you do this, Jeannie? Did you?

She tries to subtly move toward the door to make an exit, but he just as subtly blocks her way.

JEANNIE: No. Why would you ask that? No, I swear. It musta been the neighbor kids or something. Maybe you left the back door open.

MAN: Jeannie, it's locked. Did you do this?

He looks at her for a moment, and then moves to the bookshelf. He glances at her to make sure she's not leaving. She's frozen in place. He moves the book and finds the necklace to be missing. He removes all the books and looks carefully. The necklace is gone.

MAN: *(cont'd)* Empty your pockets.

JEANNIE: What?

He approaches her quickly, before she can move.

MAN: You heard me.

JEANNIE: *(moving away)* You can't just boss me around any more. I'm an adult now, and...

MAN: Empty your pockets.

JEANNIE: No.

He closes distance.

JEANNIE: *(cont'd)* Stay away from me.

Holding her, checking her pockets,

MAN: If you're lying again. ... If one more time and I'm...

He finds the necklace.

MAN: *(cont'd)* Jeannie?

JEANNIE: Alright, fine, fuck it. I lied. Is that the end of the fucking world?

MAN: You're stealing your mother's necklace. You did this to the house, and you lied.

JEANNIE: I needed money. I asked you before.

MAN: You dropped out of the clinic, didn't you?

JEANNIE: Let me go. I need money. Gimme some money. You've got it and I want some. I want...

MAN: What you want is crystal meth. Right? Say it. Say it!

JEANNIE: I want crystal meth. There.

MAN: You're not leaving here.

JEANNIE: Yes I am. I'll go anywhere I fucking want and you can't stop me. Let me go.

MAN: You're not leaving, god damn it.

JEANNIE: I can do anything I god damn want and if you don't give me money for drugs, then I'll earn it on the street. Get it? 'Cause there's plenty of old men who'll give me a hundred bucks for a blow job. Rim their ass and it's an extra hundred. Spread my pussy lips for some photos, another hundred. Oh, I can get money and I fucking will.

MAN: *(desperate)* Why do you want to ruin everything? Jeannie, look at you.

He drags her to the mirror.

MAN: *(cont'd)* Will you look in the mirror? You're running out of life. You are. Look at yourself.

JEANNIE: Don't talk to me about life. You never spent time with mom or me. It's always about your patients, your practice...

MAN *(overlapping, sarcastically)* Well I'm sorry for wanting to help people, make a living. Excuse me.

JEANNIE: *(continuing)* ...somebody's nose job, or cheek implants or botox fucking lips. So don't tell me...

MAN: I know where this goes. Some day, I'll get a call and you'll be gone. Dead. ... An O.D., a car accident, some tough guy beats you up. It's right there, don't you see it? And I don't want that. Let me help you. I love you and I'll be there for you and your mother.

JEANNIE: *(immediately, flatly)* I need money. Do I get it from you, or selling tricks? ... Well?

He slowly extracts cash from his pocket. She starts to take the hundred dollar bills, but he slowly and deliberately tears them into shreds.

MAN: Money doesn't mean anything now. I don't have money anymore. I only have you and your mom.

JEANNIE: *(leaving)* No, dad, you don't. You only have mom.

Jeannie walks out, leaving her dad behind. After a moment,

MAN: *(sotto)* I am not going to let that happen.

Regular Guys

AN UNDERGROUND SUBWAY STATION – *It's nearly 11:30 p.m.. A few people sit on benches or stand and wait for the subway. A man, WILLIAM DANIELS, mid 40s, sits. A WOMAN, mid-20s, Chinese, pleasant, walks in and sits off to the side. She carries a Purse, takes out a paperback Novel and reads. Daniels checks his watch. Another man, "PHIL", mid-40s, athletic but otherwise a regular guy, walks into the subway staging area, carrying a Newspaper. A subway train pulls into the station.*

Two or more people get on, including someone on the bench with Daniels.

A few people get off the subway and walk through the station and leave.

Phil sits down on the bench and opens the Newspaper. The Woman with the Novel glances up, then continues reading. There's a moment of silence. Daniels glances at his watch again.

DANIELS: The subway trains always run late here.

PHIL: Oh?

DANIELS: They run late. Five minutes, sometimes six. ... Usually five minutes.

PHIL: They do that.

DANIELS: And it's late again tonight.

PHIL: What time do you have?

DANIELS: *(looks at watch again)* Eleven-thirty.

PHIL: Long day.

DANIELS: Very long, you don't even...and tedious. Mentally... exhausting.

PHIL: Nothing's easy anymore, I know that much. *(turns to Daniels)* The name's Phil.

He extends his hand. Daniels takes it and they shake.

DANIELS: William Daniels. ... Bill. I go by Bill.

PHIL: Okay then, good. ... Bill. *(laughs)* Phil and Bill, workaholic subway junkies.

A long silence. Another train comes in. Daniels gets up to look. Phil moves with Daniels as Daniels looks, but it's the wrong train. Phil sits back on the bench as Daniels does. The rest of the people in the station, except the Woman reading the novel, get up and board the train. No one gets off.

PHIL: *(cont'd)* You catch the ball game today? On the radio?

DANIELS: No, I didn't...Well, no. They won. Did they win?

PHIL: Oh yeah! Great game. Metzger pitched six, struck out nine. And Davenport, he hits a dinger in the fifth. ... That guy.

DANIELS: Davenport?

PHIL: Rookie. Oh yeah, he's comin' along.

DANIELS: I don't get a chance...Things have been complica[ted]...Hectic.

PHIL: Well, you gotta smell the flowers. *(off his look)* You know, take time out. Roar a the crowd, hot dogs, peanuts. Take in the game. 'Cause you never know.

DANIELS: Yeah, I've been wanting to...What do you mean?

PHIL: What?

DANIELS: "'Cause you never know"?

PHIL: Nothin'. That? Figure of speech. "You never know"... You could go a full season...

DANIELS: Oh.

PHIL: ...go a full season and not see one game.

DANIELS: Oh yeah, right. You never know.

Silence again. Daniels looks around and sees no one to his right. He's nervous. Then he looks to his left and behind and sees the Woman. He's quietly relieved.

PHIL: So, "Bill," what is it that you do?

DANIELS: Me? ... I'm an accountant. ... Well, not an accountant. A **bookkeeper** actually.

PHIL: Bookkeeper. Sounds...very, detailed. Is it detailed?

DANIELS: *(relaxed, opening up)* Oh, I suppose...but it can be rewarding. *(catches the double meaning)*...in a **business** sense, professionally. A professional sense.

PHIL: *(beat)* I can see that. Rewarding. I bet it can. You work with client money, do you? In your bookkeeping? Or is it all just numbers.

Daniels is nervous again.

DANIELS: Numbers. I keep records, that's all. ... Sometimes, I make deposits...but I don't have any money on me, if that's...

PHIL: No, I didn't mean...

DANIELS: *(overlapping)*...if that's what you're saying.

PHIL: I wasn't saying...But sure, you got the responsibilities, with somebody's money.

DANIELS: *(defensive)* Several clients, actually.

PHIL: Right.

DANIELS: It's a big opportunity for someone like...What I mean is, that's not what I meant.

PHIL: Opportunity...for growth?

DANIELS: Right. ... Not **my** growth.

PHIL: No, I wouldn't say. Were you saying that?

DANIELS: *(flatly)* I keep the books.

PHIL: That's what you told me.

DANIELS: *(changing the subject)* What do, what do you do?

PHIL: Me. Oh I'm...a facilitator.

DANIELS: What does that...

PHIL: *(interrupts)* I facilitate solutions.

DANIELS: Oh.

PHIL: Like, for example, something gets out of hand, and the options...or let's say, the alternatives, have been, explored. So...

DANIELS: *(interjecting)*...they call you.

PHIL: *(friendly)* That's right! Very good. They call me.

DANIELS: *(beat)* Who are "they," your clients?

PHIL: Guys. Just regular guys, like me and you...

DANIELS: I see.

PHIL: *(overlapping)*...but these guys, they are persistent. It's... personal to them. It becomes personal.

Daniels gets up.

DANIELS: *(panicking)* Look, if this is about...

Phil grabs Daniels' arm and firmly sits him down, letting go as Daniels stays put.

PHIL: No, relax. Bill, Bill. You know, it's not about anything. Go ahead an' relax.

Daniels remains seated, but is starting to freak out.

DANIELS: I don't have to sit here and take this.

PHIL: No you don't. You could stand up and walk away. Right now. Or, you could make me happy, sit here and deal with this.

DANIELS: I am an honest man.

PHIL: In which case, you got nothin' to worry about. You know, my daddy, he used to tell me, "The truth will set you free." *(laughs)* I always liked that idea". ...will set you free."

DANIELS: *(meekly)* Leave me alone. ... Please don't...

PHIL: *(quietly)*...hurt you? Bill, I'm surprised. You think I'd do that? Hurt you, right here, with a witness watching?

Daniels glances over to see the Woman keeping an eye on things. He relaxes again, slightly.

DANIELS: Who are you?

PHIL: I'm nobody. And I'm everybody. Now I want you to listen to me. I'm gonna ask you a question, and you think about it. Real careful. Okay?

Daniels nods.

PHIL: *(cont'd)* These opportunities we were talking about...the rewards you took...from your "hard work" *(beat)* Are any of them, left?

Daniels doesn't answer.

PHIL: *(cont'd) (upbeat)* You know, if you wanted...just say you wanted, to give them back, to a particular employer from whom you took them...*(quiet intensity)* Are there, any, left? ...

Tell the truth.

Daniels wants to lie, but he fears the consequences of lying worse than he fears the truth. Finally,

DANIELS: *(defeated)* No. ... I spent it all.

PHIL: You spent...Oh, oh now see, see that's too bad. You spent all of it. ... I didn't, I really didn't want to hear that.

Another train is coming in. Phil stands but Daniels does not. Phil leaves his Newspaper on the bench.

PHIL: *(cont'd)* Hey what do you know, there's our train. Just like you said, five minutes late. You coming?

DANIELS: *(without looking up)* No.

PHIL: Okay, suit yourself. *(upbeat)* How 'bout the ball park tomorrow? You goin'? It's a day game. Double header...

Daniels doesn't speak, and keeps his head down. If he just stays put, he figures he'll be alright. Phil discreetly glances to the Woman and makes eye contact with her. Does he nod? She resumes her reading.

PHIL: *(cont'd)* If you can make it, you should go. ... 'Cause you never know.

Phil steps onto the subway, which pulls out. Phil looks back to the station, receding away. Daniels almost collapses on the bench, his head now in his hands. He's crying. He has forgotten the Woman, but she hasn't forgotten him.

She walks over to him, and with a handkerchief, removes a PISTOL from her purse. Without even a trace of emotion, she

SHOOTS HIM ONCE IN THE HEAD.

Daniels falls over, very much dead.

WOMAN: *(Chinese accent)* That "truth set you free" crap? Bad advice. No good.

The Woman leaves the pistol and handkerchief on the bench.

WOMAN: *(walking off)* Better to lie guts out. *(sarcastic)* "Set you free."

The Newspaper HEADLINES chronicle another gangland slaying.

Ring, The

AT THE COUNTY DISTRICT ATTORNEY'S OFFICES – *a sharp Deputy District Attorney, KATHY MERCER, late 20s to early 30s, sits at her desk, momentarily avoiding the inevitable – another emotionally draining visit with the distraught father of murder victim Marcie Parker. After several moments, she hits the intercom.*

KATHY: *(to the intercom)* I can see Mr. Parker now.

VOICE: *(on the intercom)* I'll send him right back.

Moments later, STEVE PARKER, late-40s, enters her office. She stands to greet him.

KATHY: *(upbeat)* Hi, come in. I was on the phone. Come on in. How ya doin'?

PARKER: Fine. I'm good. I've been okay. Nice to see you.

KATHY: So, the preliminary hearing is coming up next week.

PARKER: Okay.

KATHY: And, I think everything will go okay, no real problems.

PARKER: Good.

KATHY: Ah, we did get a 1538.5 –

Pronounced, "fifteen thirty-eight point five."

KATHY: *(continuing)* – motion to suppress evidence – served on us today.

PARKER: They, ah...

KATHY: Right.

PARKER: They can do that?

KATHY: Yes.

PARKER: Oh, okay, but what evidence would that pertain...

KATHY: Well, the, the blanket...*(beat)*...in the trunk, so there's the car search. The defendant's car. We shouldn't be talking about this.

Parker's in trouble already. He's crying.

PARKER: Wait...Okay, I'll be okay.

KATHY: Okay.

She puts her hand on his shoulder, and hands him a tissue. Kathy then sits down to wait this out. Her head down. She waits.

PARKER: Okay, I'm okay.

KATHY: So, there's a chance we might lose the blanket evidence, which is the most direct evidence that ties the dirt bag to the vic's...I'm sorry, your **daughter's** murder, but there's some other circumstantial evidence we would still have.

PARKER: The search of the car was bad?

KATHY: There's an issue of exigent circumstances. It could go either way.

PARKER: Okay.

KATHY: But the rest of the evidence was seized by search warrant, and thank god, the blanket evidence doesn't appear in the application for warrant.

PARKER: That's a lucky break, right?

KATHY: Right. So whatever we found on his person, which wasn't a lot, and at his apartment, that's solid. See that's admissible.

PARKER: Okay, well that's good news. I remember you telling me something about that, you know, before when I saw you. A couple of times before.

KATHY: Yeah, I remember. You're doing better today than then.

They smile.

PARKER: I'm trying.

KATHY: Benson, in Writs and Appeals, he wrote up the warrant affidavit. It's solid.

PARKER: Oh yeah. I hear he's a good lawyer.

Then, referring to the defendant,

PARKER: *(cont'd)* Why did he do this? She was only fifteen. Did you know we were going to Sea World the next day? She loved Sea World.

KATHY: I didn't know that. She looked like a very nice girl.

PARKER: Oh, she was. She would have liked you. She talked about being a lawyer. ... *(he's lost in tears)* I'm sorry. I shouldn't come here.

It's tough on Kathy, too, to see this suffering.

KATHY: No...It's, well it's tough, you know, to see you cry, and I know how important and all it is for you. ... I want to keep you informed.

PARKER: Thank you. ... So, will Mr. Benson be there for the motion to suppress, at the preliminary hearing?

KATHY: No, he's actually over at South Court, supervising that office now. But I had Writs work up some P&As for me, I'll be filing that tomorrow.

PARKER: Okay, okay. So the case looks good?

KATHY: He's got this phony alibi story, claims he was out of the State, but we've got our investigators out there trying to break it down.

PARKER: Okay.

Kathy gets up to usher Parker out. She has a lot of work to do and the meeting's winding down. Walking him to the door,

KATHY: So, if anything new comes up...

PARKER: *(interrupting)* Kathy, I remembered something...

She stops.

KATHY: What's that?

PARKER: Earlier, you asked me what Marcie was wearing on that day...

KATHY: Yeah?

PARKER: She may have had a ring with her.

Still not seeing a connection,

KATHY: A ring?

PARKER: Well, a boy at school had given it to her. They wanted a relationship. We told her, my wife and I told her, after a talk, that she was too young to wear a ring.

Kathy walks him back to her desk.

KATHY: Oh.

PARKER: She couldn't wear it. See, that's why, when you asked what she was wearing, I didn't think...

KATHY: But you didn't take the ring from her?

PARKER: She took it off, and I looked at it. It was...

KATHY: *(interrupting)* They found a ring.

PARKER: *(not hearing her)* I looked at it and...

KATHY: *(interrupting)* They found...The Sheriff's office found a ring in his bureau. In the defendant's fucking bureau. They couldn't ID it.

PARKER: I saw the ring she'd been given, and I know who... gave it to her.

Kathy starts feverishly writing notes on a legal pad.

KATHY: He told Sheriff's investigators his grandmother gave it to him. She's dead, so there's no way to refute that story. We thought there was no way. Can you describe...Wait, wait a minute.

She grabs a TAPE RECORDER and punches "RECORD".

KATHY: *(cont'd)* I want to get this on tape. *(to the tape recorder)* This is Deputy District Attorney Kathy Mercer. It's Wednesday, July 3, 2002. I'm interviewing Steve Parker concerning the death of his daughter Marcie. *(to Parker)* Mr. Parker, was there a ring which your daughter was given before her death?

PARKER: *(slowly, deliberately)* Yes. From a young boy at school.

KATHY: And you saw this ring?

PARKER: I did. We looked at it the first day. Her mother and I told her she shouldn't wear it. She was too young, but that it was alright to keep it with her.

KATHY: Could you describe it? Describe the ring.

PARKER: It was silver and had a red colored flower ornament on it, and it had an inscription on the inside. It said, it said, "True love lives forever."

Kathy puts her hand to her mouth, realizing that this is now truly a key piece of prosecution evidence.

KATHY: And when was the last time you saw Marcie in possession of the ring?

PARKER: The day she died, she was starting to leave the house. She came back into the kitchen, said "I forgot my ring," and grabbed it off the kitchen counter. I saw her pick it up. That's the last time I... *(distraught)* My baby didn't come home.

Kathy punches "Save" to save the recording, then clicks off the recorder.

KATHY: Mr. Parker, I've looked at the ring they found in Dave Davidson's bureau, and it is...exactly the ring you just described.

PARKER: That motherfucker. I'll kill him myself. That fucking motherfucker!

KATHY: You won't have to, we've got him now. This directly ties him to the scene and to the victim, contradicts his story and impeaches his alibi. He's going down for murder one.

He gets up and puts his arms around her.

PARKER: Oh, that's so good. I'm so happy, you don't know what it's like. Nobody knows what it's like.

Road to Daisyville

RIDING ALONG IN A CHEVY TRUCK – *a MAN and a WOMAN. The passenger's a pretty girl, mid-20s, in jeans and short tee-shirt, carrying a large handbag. The driver's in his 40s, wearing jeans, tee-shirt and a tattered baseball cap. They're in the middle of a tense moment.*

MAN: I didn't mean anything by it.

WOMAN: I thought it was weird, okay?

MAN: Okay.

WOMAN: *(explaining)* You don't have to not talk. I just don't want you to talk about me is all.

MAN: Okay.

They drive along.

WOMAN: You really think my hair is pretty?

MAN: I shouldn't talk about that or you'll think I'm weird.

WOMAN: Right.

MAN: *(beat)* Yes.

WOMAN: *(upset)* See, that's what I mean, I knew you'd talk about it!

MAN: *(overlapping)* You asked me...

WOMAN: *(continuing)* And I know what I asked you but you're supposed to know better.

MAN: Women.

WOMAN: Men.

MAN: How far d'you say you're going?

WOMAN: I said down the road a ways.

MAN: Well, I'm going to Beecher, in case you're going farther than that.

WOMAN: Okay.

MAN: Are you?

WOMAN: Mind your driving. ... I'm going to Daisyville.

MAN: Daisyville? You running from something?

WOMAN: No, next question.

MAN: To something?

WOMAN: No. Two down, six to go.

MAN: What's this, a game?

WOMAN: Yes, and you're not very good. Three down, five to go.

MAN: *(gruff)* I don't like games. ... Are you leaving for good?

WOMAN: That's two questions.

MAN: Are you leaving something?

WOMAN: I'd have to say...no with an explanation.

But she gives no explanation.

MAN: You can't say that. You gotta give the explanation.

WOMAN: Yes or no questions only. Four down, four to go.

MAN: I got four left? Don't answer that. *(slyly)* Are you happy to be going where you're going?

WOMAN: *(brightening up)* Yes! Three to go.

MAN: So how come I've never seen you around before?

She sits mute.

MAN: *(cont'd)* You must live out of town, 'cause I'd know if I'd seen you around. ... This is impossible.

WOMAN: Do you want a hint?

MAN: Yes.

WOMAN: Everything worth having is right here in my bag.

MAN: Oh, you got money in there.

WOMAN: No, and you're losing. Two to go.

MAN: *(overlapping)* Well I didn't know. You said it was valuables.

WOMAN: Everything worth having.

MAN: I hate this game.

He sees a ranch in the distance. Pointing it out.

MAN: *(cont'd)* That's where I'm headed. The Sullivan ranch.

WOMAN: Oh, you work on a ranch?

MAN: *(amused)* Nope. One down, six to go.

WOMAN: You're playing the game, not me.

MAN: *(overlapping)* I give up.

WOMAN: If you give up, I get out.

MAN: Shit.

WOMAN: And no cussing.

MAN: Fine. ... Your sister had a baby and there's baby clothes in there that it grew out of and she gave 'em to you in case you're ever pregnant?

WOMAN: Nooo. Where'd that come from?

MAN: I don't even know what I'm trying to guess.

WOMAN: Why I'm going where I'm going.

MAN: *(sarcastic)* Oh well that clears it all up.

WOMAN: One to go and I'm outta here.

MAN: I've never heard of Daisyville.

WOMAN: Another hint: *(whispers)* It's a mythical place.

MAN: Well how do you do that? How do you go somewhere doesn't exist?

WOMAN: That's not a "yes or no", and if I told you that, you'd know why I'm going there.

MAN: So I gotta figure out why you're going someplace that doesn't exist, with everything worth having in that little bag…?

WOMAN: *(overlapping)* Yes!

MAN: *(continuing)* …and you're not leaving something, though you're happy to be going, and I've never seen you before, though, as you do admit, you have pretty hair.

WOMAN: Compliment noted.

MAN: *(beat)* Can I ask a question that doesn't count against me? And don't answer if it does! Are there family photos in your purse?

WOMAN: *Yes!*

MAN: *(confident)* You got pictures of your parents in there and you're going on an adventure!

WOMAN: *(smiling)* Yes, yes! How'd you know?

MAN: You had trouble saying if you were leaving something behind, which sounds like somebody died and you have their pictures, and it's probably parents, 'cause I went through that too. And I figured if you're going to an imaginary place, it's gotta be some kind of adventure!

WOMAN: *(pleased)* See, we're connecting here.

MAN: Don't think I've never done an adventure. Never much made it out of Bakersfield.

She pulls her hair back away from her face. He drives to the side of the road at a dirt crossroads.

MAN: *(cont'd)* So, this is where I turn. *(smiles)* I wasn't, I wasn't going to Daisyville today.

WOMAN: You could go to Daisyville with me.

MAN: That's a crazy idea. ... That's a crazy idea.

WOMAN: You said that.

MAN: I can't just pick up...

WOMAN: I'm headed there now, and I like you. It feels right. So, if you want to go, you could.

MAN: I could? I could go with you?

She smiles and nods her head.

WOMAN: Together.

He's finally found the one.

MAN: I waited a long time, you know. For you.

They embrace. She kisses him. The adventure's already started.

Safe at Home

AFTERNOON AT A BASEBALL DIAMOND – *a young man, FRANK, 40s, stands at bat in a game-worn baseball uniform. WE SEE his head and shoulders from behind and to the side. It could be a real game.*

FRANK: *(sotto, in "Announcer's Voice")* Pitcher gets the sign. A two-two ball game, two outs. The wind-up and...

Frank swings an imaginary bat, "hits" the ball and runs for First Base, in what we NOW SEE is an empty baseball field.

FRANK: *(cont'd)* What a shot, a rope to left field. Drummond cruises into First Base with a clean single.

A woman, KATIE, attractive in late 20s, early 30s is seen off the field, watching. She's wearing shorts and a halter top and carries a BOTTLE OF WATER.

FRANK: *(cont'd)* He may go for the steal. Pitcher's got a slow move to the plate.

Frank takes his lead off First Base.

FRANK: *(cont'd)* Drummond steps off. One step, two, he's out to the grass. The pitch...

Frank breaks for Second Base,

FRANK: *(cont'd)* Gravallo's got it, sets, the throw to Second...

He dives into the bag. It's a dusty mess. Lying face down in the dirt,

FRANK: *(cont'd)* He's safe! Safe! That's steal number twenty-two on the season, putting the go-ahead run in scoring position. (This really puts the pressure on Dixon.)

Frank dusts himself off, tipping his hat to the "crowd". Katie walks out to the field.

KATIE: Can I play?

FRANK: Oh, hi. I didn't see you there.

She walks toward him. Standing off from Second, she offers her water bottle.

KATIE: Want some water?

Frank starts to walk to her, then retreats to the "bag", smiling.

FRANK: You're trying to pull me off the bag, aren't you? Oldest trick in the book.

She walks over and hands him the water, which he gulps down.

KATIE: I've seen you around. Frank, right?

Frank nods his head. She gets the water bottle back and walks away toward the mound. Frank takes a lead off Second Base.

FRANK: And you're...Katie. Cute shorts.

KATIE: You better get your mind back on the game...*(she turns)* Shortstop might sneak up on you!

Frank dives back for Second Base.

KATIE: *(cont'd)* I said he might sneak up on you. Fact is, he's camping out at deep short.

Frank stands up indignantly, dusting himself off.

FRANK: I saw him. The Pitcher made a move is all.

KATIE: *(doing her own "Announcer" voice)* This Frank kid... (What was your last name again?) That's right, Drummond. Well folks, he could be seeing his last days at the Show. How old is he anyway? Course, he is kind of cute...So, Third Base coach flashes the signs. *(she mimes flashing the signs)* Drummond takes a lead. It's not much of a lead though. Well, for his age bracket...Pitcher looks, and the pitch.

Frank takes off for Third.

KATIE: *(cont'd)* Ohhh, it's a pitchout. Snap throw to Third Base...

Frank looks at Katie, in a "Who's team are you on?"-look and throws on the brakes.

KATIE: *(cont'd)* They've got him in a pickle. ... And with those wheels, well this could be our third out. Throw to Second Base...

Back and forth Katie "runs" Frank, exhausting him.

KATIE: *(cont'd)* And to Third...back to shortstop, to Third, catcher's in the play now, to Second, to catcher (there's a good looking hunk), to Second, oh he fumbles the ball, the throw, Drummond dives into Third Base! It's gonna be close!

FRANK: He's safe.

KATIE: *(overlapping)* The dust is settling, and...he's, **out** at Third!

FRANK: I cannot be out. I slid under the tag. Right under.

KATIE: I call the play-by-play and you're out.

FRANK: He dropped the ball.

KATIE: After the tag.

FRANK: Tag was late. I touched the bag.

KATIE: Tag, then touch. Tag touch. Ba-dum.

FRANK: But the bag's way out here.

He indicates how the "bag" extends far inside the Baseline.

KATIE: *(laughing)* The bag isn't that big. You men, you're always overestimating size. ... You're out at Third, now you wanna be outta the game?

They're nose to nose. He kicks a little dirt on her tennies.

FRANK: Safe.

KATIE: Last warning. You're out at Third.

FRANK: *(beat)* Pansy.

KATIE: You're outta here! Outta the game. Finissimo. Caput. Hit the bricks buster. History, done deal.

FRANK: Katie, hold on. I really wanted to steal home.

KATIE: Too bad, 'cause the game's over for you, Buster.

FRANK: I was gonna slide in right under Gravallo's nose.

KATIE: No can do. And you better be nice, or I just might umpire all your games.

FRANK: Not, that.

KATIE: That. Big-time that.

FRANK: Come on, let me steal home one time.

Katie carefully considers this. Then,

KATIE: Alright, steal home

Frank sets up his lead off Third Base.

FRANK: Coach flashes the signs, which Drummond expertly picks up. The crowd is hushed. Drummond is taking a dangerous lead. What could he be thinking? ... Could this be, a hit-and-run? ... Gravallo sets up in his patented-but-antiquated duck-walk, low-brow squat...

KATIE: Okay, enough about Gravallo's squat.

FRANK: There's a steely-eyed glare from Dixon, which Drummond fires right back. What a match up, what a duel. But with Big-Jim-Paxton at the plate. Oh he's a threat for the long ball, but what a strike-out king! Drummond stretches his lead. That Frank Drummond, what a guy, what bravado, what a team player...

KATIE: What a crock.

FRANK: It's like time-stands-still. We see it now in slo-mo, *(slow, deep voice)* Dixon makes his patented slow-as-molasses-in-winter move to the plate...*(in pseudo "slow motion")* And Frank breaks for home. *(Did he tip his cap?)*...It's the Suicide Squeeze! Crowd's on its feet, the pitch is away, sailing, speeding, sliding towards its destiny in Gravallo's meaty, mulish, morose grasp.

KATIE: I think I'm gonna throw up.

FRANK: Big Jim Paxton takes the stride. He swings. Ummmph! Wooof! It's a miss. Paxton missed the ball! Paxton missed the ball! ... Frank's starting to dive, I think he's got it, will he?

Frank now "returns" to normal speed, springs forward and dives into home plate.

KATIE: You're out! Out of there. He tagged you and you're out!

FRANK: I was calling the play-by-play this time.

KATIE: And I was the Home Plate Umpire, and I called you out! *(sticks her tongue out at him)* Judgment call, no appeal, you lose.

FRANK: I feel cheated.

KATIE: Write your Congressman.

FRANK: Come on Blue.

KATIE: *(overlapping)* Now hit the showers.

FRANK: The showers?

KATIE: That's right. Wet, cold, no towel, showers. Burrrr.

FRANK: *(taunting)* You gonna make me?

She presses up against him now.

KATIE: I-think-I-owe-it to the fans. Make sure you clean up your act.

FRANK: You push pretty hard.

KATIE: *(glancing down)* I was thinking the same thing.

Their "argument" deteriorates into a kiss. Then, moments later, they walk off the field together.

FRANK: You said I could steal home.

KATIE: I didn't say you'd be safe. (Did I say you'd be safe?) And you were out.

FRANK: I just wanted to be safe.

KATIE: At home?

FRANK: Yeah.

KATIE: You got that.

FRANK: So, what's for dinner tonight?

KATIE: Your favorite.

Second Chance

INSIDE A DOUBLE-WIDE TRAILER – *are JOE, a man in his 40s and TAMMY, his old lady (younger, early 20s), as they drink beers and watch TV.*

TAMMY: You think we can ever get us one a them four-wheel drive trucks?

JOE: Long as they still sell 'em to white trash.

They laugh.

TAMMY: There any beers left, Joe?

JOE: I think one's in the fridge.

TAMMY: Be a sweetheart an' get it for me, will ya?

JOE: I am way too comfortable, baby.

TAMMY: I'll give you a blow job later.

JOE: *(getting up immediately)* Bottle or frosted mug?

TAMMY: Very funny.

Joe grabs a beer from the fridge and a bag of chips.

JOE: Honey, where's that green onion dip?

TAMMY: We ran out last night. The boys were over, 'member?

JOE: Sure, you're right.

Joe hands her a beer, puts some chips on the coffee table, and lies face-down in her lap.

TAMMY: Get your face outta there unless you're prepared to do the nasty.

JOE: And you know I am.

TAMMY: *(pulling him up)* Joe, you know what?

JOE: What?

TAMMY: Let's have a baby.

Joe immediately sits up, stone-faced.

JOE: We talked about that. I got two kids, both old as you, an' I'm done with that shit.

TAMMY: You'd be a good dad.

JOE: I was a good dad. Been there, done that. Conversation closed.

TAMMY: "Conversation closed!" You always say that. I wanna talk an' it's "conversation closed."

JOE: We're not gettin' into this, Tammy. Let's just watch the tube.

TAMMY: Well I'm gettin' into it 'cause I'm twenty-three an' I ain't gettin' any younger an' I wanna get knocked up.

JOE: Well you ain't gettin' knocked up by me!

TAMMY: If that's the way you want it, fine.

JOE: Which is supposed to mean?

TAMMY: Whatever.

JOE: Is supposed to mean what?!

TAMMY: Figure it out.

JOE: Don't you go fuckin' around on me...

TAMMY: Watch your mouth.

JOE: You go fuckin' around, I'll leave your ass.

TAMMY: Watch your god damn mouth!

JOE: Don't be fuckin' around.

TAMMY: I'll do what I god damned please.

JOE: Let's have our beers an' just drop it.

TAMMY: We ain't gonna drop nothin' or drink no more beers. Shit! I want to start a family, Joe. Is that such a bad thing?

JOE: No, it's not bad...

TAMMY: *(sadly)* You don't think I'd be a right mother, is that it?

JOE: No, no you'd be a damn right mother, no doubt.

TAMMY: So, you don't love me or what?

JOE: I love you so much. I watch you at night, when you sleep, an' I don't know how I got so fucking lucky to have you. I love you baby.

TAMMY: *(tenderly)* You do?

JOE: You know I do. ... I just...it's only...I don't know if I can do "kids" again.

TAMMY: I'd be there too. We'd do the kid thing together.

JOE: Yeah.

TAMMY: I'd get up mosta the time an' it won't be no bother, the crying.

JOE: That ain't it. I mean, I don't mind.

TAMMY: What is it then Joe? Why do you wanna break my heart? I love you so much. I look at you I wanna jump your bones. I like your touch...*(kidding him)* An' for an old guy, you're a pretty good kisser.

JOE: *(laughs)* My lips ain't gone sour yet!

TAMMY: So...

JOE: So, I already lost my kids once.

TAMMY: I know.

JOE: The Court gave my ex full custody and let her move up north. The kids, you know, they didn't want to leave their dad, but...They'd call an' text me and so on, 'cause you know, for years it was the only...I did get a couple of weeks in the summer with 'em. *(losing it)* So that's been good.

TAMMY: I love you Joe.

JOE: You wouldn't hurt me like she did?

TAMMY: I would never leave you, not for no reason. You're a kind, gentle, an' sexy man.

JOE: Do you really love me?

TAMMY: I love you so much, I do.

JOE: *(long pause)* I wouldn't have kids with you Tammy...if we wasn't **married** first.

TAMMY: You wanna marry me?

JOE: Will you marry me and have our child?

TAMMY: ...maybe two?

JOE: That'd be okay by me.

TAMMY: Then I do, or I will. I will marry you Joe Hooper, and I will stay with you and our three kids forever and a day.

JOE: *(softly)* How'd it wind up **three** all of a sudden?

TAMMY: *(kissing him)* Shut up Joe, an' let's get started.

Seduction

INSIDE A REMOTE MOUNTAIN CABIN AT NIGHT –
where a U.S. Marshal, TINA, is making coffee. A blizzard howls outside in the darkness as SAM, a protected witness informant, enters from another room. He wears a jacket.

SAM: I couldn't sleep. Rest a the Marshals are dead to the world.

Tina looks over, sharply.

SAM: *(cont'd)* They're **asleep**. Relax.

She sits down with her coffee at the window. He follows.

SAM: *(cont'd)* How's a broad like you get interested in being a U.S. Marshal?

TINA: *(pause)* I wanted to track down the bad guys.

SAM: And I'm one of 'em, right?

TINA: Yeah.

SAM: So it doesn't affect your sense of sensibilities you protecting a bad guy?

TINA: You're a federal witness. Personally, I rather put a bullet in your head.

SAM: Don't pull no punches.

TINA: No offense, but you're strictly an assignment to me. You ought to be going to prison, for life. Instead, your boss'll do the time. It's a trade off.

SAM: No offense, but you're being a little offensive, you know.

TINA: It is what it is.

SAM: *(looking out the window)* Glad I'm inside tonight.

TINA: You **hear** about storms like this. ... We're in the mouth of a monster.

SAM: I was in the mountains one other time. Whacked out a guy in the Catskills. Accountant who got careless with some decimal points.

TINA: *(indicating)* Then he got four shots to the head.

SAM: The "Double Deuce."

TINA: Right.

SAM: Thou shall not fucking steal from the Gallini family.

TINA: *(pause)* How'd you become a contract killer?

SAM: *(smiles slightly)* One day you're leanin' on deadbeats to pay the juice, the next you're whackin' guys out.

TINA: Just like that?

SAM: I thought about bein' a cop. When I was growin' up. Do good things for people. Make 'em like me. A little respect's all I wanted. Eleven years old, I'm selling newspapers in the neighborhood, block after block, bustin' my ass, but nobody buys.

TINA: There's lots of reasons [they wouldn't buy]...

SAM: *(interrupting)* So, I break windows. Relentless. ... I tell 'em, "You buy the newspaper, nobody breaks your windows no more." I get subscriptions up the ying yang. Every-fucking-body wants to buy. Everybody. I had my respect.

TINA: *(sarcastic)* That's very heart-warming.

SAM: *(smiles slightly)* It is what it is. *(serious)* You know, you don't mind me sayin', you've got it goin' in the looks department. Very beautiful.

TINA: *(flatly)* Thanks.

SAM: I ain't been around no decent broads. Don't know how to talk to 'em much.

TINA: You're doing alright.

SAM: I'm good at trash talk. It's nice speaking to a classy lady for a change.

Tina smiles slightly, and keeps looking out the window.

SAM: *(cont'd)* I wouldn't know to say, for example, I like the way you smell. Perfume, shampoo...

TINA: It must be the lotion.

SAM: The lotion. And your hair looks soft. Can I touch it?

She's uncomfortable but doesn't pull away as he touches.

SAM: *(cont'd)* See, my neighborhood, broads – women – they let themselves go. You, you set a good example.

TINA: I wouldn't know.

SAM: My mother was a prostitute. My old man, a number at California Men's Colony. I never had no real...Whadayacallit? Role model.

TINA: People change.

SAM: *(laughs)* I turned out like this. I ain't much to look at.

TINA: I've seen worse.

SAM: I always wondered, if things was different, what I coulda done in life.

TINA: Probably a lot.

SAM: Maybe I coulda had a family or somethin'. ... You got a family?

TINA: Not yet, no.

SAM: *(nods)* I know I ain't worth much to nobody. People, women don't want me.

TINA: *(pause)* You're good looking. Plenty of women would be attracted to you.

SAM: If I was legit, right?

TINA: Well...

SAM: Prostitutes maybe. No, I'm a fuckin' piece-a-shit. You

know it, I know it, the god damned jury's gonna know it. Worthless fucking garbage.

TINA: You're not garbage. Sam, don't...Sam, look at me. You're worth something, to somebody. Your life's about to start over. A new identity, a job. You got a chance now.

SAM: Nah, I won't fit in, not with a babe like you.

His head's in his hands. Tina watches him, and then,

TINA: Come here. Sam, come here.

He turns and she leans into him slowly. She kisses him lightly, but he doesn't respond.

TINA: *(cont'd)* See, that's not so tough.

SAM: *(distraught)* You're just doing it, make me feel normal. For the testimony thing. Nobody wants me.

TINA: *(softly)* They do. Sam, they...Come here.

She draws him in and kisses him passionately.

SAM: *(kissing, caressing)* Like this? ... Okay, okay. Maybe you're right. Maybe I ain't so repugnant after all.

The passion builds. She's losing herself. Suddenly, he extracts her gun from its holster, steps back and trains the weapon on her.

SAM: *(cont'd)* Do you want me **now**? Get up, 'cause you and I are walkin' outta this shit hole. I ain't testifying against nobody.

TINA: There's three feet of snow. It's ten degrees.

He tosses her jacket to her.

SAM: Put this on.

She slips on her jacket.

SAM: *(cont'd)* You think I'm stupid? No, see I ain't some patsy with a target on his head waitin' to be whacked out. We're outta here, an' you make a sound, you're fucking dead.

He grabs her by the hair, she complies and they walk outside into the blizzard conditions.

Umbrella

EXT. STREET – RETAIL DISTRICT – BUSINESS HOURS

On a bright sunny warm day, a man, JIMMY, 40s, sits on a bus bench, talking to himself. We see him from a bit of a distance, very excited. As we get closer, we hear him cheering on a baseball team – the Yankees. Mickey Mantle is about to come to bat.

JIMMY: Put him in. Put in the slugger! Let him up to bat.

Slowly, we begin to HEAR the sounds of "the ball game." But it's present day and Jimmy wears no earphones. He's dressed in shabby clothes that have seen many nights on the streets. A dirty worn jacket sits beside him on the bench. The baseball sounds he hears are in his mind.

A store CLERK, late 20s to mid-30s, female, walks out of a nearby retail store and picks up a compact black umbrella, buttoned closed by a strap. Spotting Jimmy, she approaches him.

CLERK: 'Scuse me, I think you dropped this. ... Sir?

He looks, momentarily breaking from his reality. The game noise we hear begins to fade and is replaced by NORMAL CITY SOUNDS. His expression drops, confused.

JIMMY: What?

CLERK: Your umbrella. You dropped it outside the store here.

He takes it from her, setting it on the bench. Then, the SOUNDS OF BASEBALL come back. He looks toward the street and the game is back for him. Jimmy "calls" the game in his "Announcer" voice.

JIMMY: *(Announcer Voice)* I think we have a substitution. A pinch hitter. The crowd's on its feet.

Jimmy stands and steps forward, but is caught by the Clerk.

CLERK: Careful, that's a busy street out there.

JIMMY: *(Announcer Voice)* Bottom of the ninth, two men on, Yankees down by two runs, deciding game of the World Series.

Jimmy sits down, and taking the arm of the Clerk, sits her down gently beside him on the bench.

JIMMY: *(cont'd)* Sit down, sit down. You're gonna miss it.

CLERK: This is a bus bench. Look, I've got to get back to work.

She starts to leave, but Jimmy's intensity stops her.

JIMMY: *(Announcer Voice)* Now batting, the slugger, the man with the golden bat. Let's see what the big man can do. *(hushed)* The crowd's settling in.

She sits again.

JIMMY: *(cont'd)* There he is! Stepping out of the dug-out. Mickey's coming to the plate, Mickey Mantle!

CLERK: *(flatly)* There he is.

JIMMY: You hear it? You hear the crowd?

Now it's from Clerk's P.O.V., and the "crowd" noise is gone and we hear the normal street sounds.

CLERK: *(flatly)* I hear it.

Clerk looks to the store, then turns to "watch" with Jimmy. We HEAR the BASEBALL SOUNDS again.

JIMMY: He's pinch hitting.

CLERK: *(somewhat enthused)* Come on Mickey. Hit that thing.

JIMMY: Oooh, that was a ball. Open your eyes umpire!

CLERK: Pitch to him now. Throw him a strike!

PEOPLE walk by, staring at the on-going spectacle, but Jimmy and the Clerk are oblivious.

JIMMY: *(springing up)* Yeah! ... He hit it, he hit it!

CLERK: *(excited)* He hit it!

JIMMY: There it goes. ... **Home run**, over the fence. At a boy Mickey! At a boy.

CLERK: He did it!

JIMMY: *(in tears)* Yankees win! I knew he could do it. I knew it. The Yankees win.

She hugs him.

JIMMY: *(cont'd)* Thanks dad, for takin' me to the game. This is the greatest day of my life.

Jimmy gives her a big hug and kiss on the cheek.

JIMMY: *(cont'd)* I love you daddy.

CLERK: *(beat)* And I love you. ... Listen, I gotta get back to work.

She gets up from the bench. The game sounds are gone now.

CLERK: *(cont'd) (softly)* Don't forget your umbrella.

JIMMY: It's gonna rain today. Clouds are dark.

The Clerk looks up at the sky. It's a beautiful sunny day.

JIMMY: *(cont'd)* Clouds are dark. It always rains now.

CLERK: *(starts to leave)* I gotta go. Bye bye.

Jimmy holds his hand out, "feeling" a rain drop.

JIMMY: See that? It gonna rain big.

CLERK: What?

We HEAR a rainstorm quickly developing.

JIMMY: There it goes! Oh, it's coming down.

She walks away. Jimmy grabs the umbrella and fumbles with the buttoned strap.

JIMMY: *(cont'd)* Wet, wet. Open umbrella.

Still fumbling and cold, he draws up his feet. We HEAR a downpour now. Jimmy's cold.

JIMMY: *(cont'd)* It's wet, I'm getting wet.

CLERK: *(helping with the strap)* I've got it.

JIMMY: Hurry. ... Thank you.

She's sitting beside him, not under the umbrella. We still hear the rain.

JIMMY: *(cont'd)* Get under.

Jimmy moves to cover her with the umbrella. People walk by, staring. A car slows down, but the JEERS of the out-of-focus young occupants are MUFFLED under the sound of rain.

JIMMY: *(cont'd)* Pull your feet up, Susie. Your daddy's gonna whip your butt if you get your tennies wet.

She pulls her feet up to the bench. Jimmy's regressing further now. We HEAR thunder and heavy rain.

JIMMY: *(cont'd)* I'm cold. Where's my mommy?

CLERK: It's okay. Look, what's your name?

JIMMY: Jimmy.

CLERK: *(spotting his jacket)* Put your jacket on.

She helps him put on his filthy jacket.

CLERK: *(cont'd)* It's alright, we'll get your mommy. We're under the umbrella, dry and warm.

He's warming up now. They're both under the umbrella.

JIMMY: Are you cold?

CLERK: No, I'm okay.

JIMMY: You can use my jacket. Here, don't be cold.

CLERK: I'm okay, thanks. ... Jimmy where do you live?

JIMMY: I live at 326 Broxton Avenue.

The rain storm goes away now. We HEAR the city streets, but muffled.

CLERK: Who do you live with?

JIMMY: *(puzzled by the question)* My mommy and daddy. ... Mommy's not home.

CLERK: *(pause)* How old are you?

JIMMY: *(holds up three fingers)* I'm four. ... Where's my mommy? ... I want daddy...They got mad.

CLERK: At you?

JIMMY: No. Yelling at mommy. They argue. Very loud. *(to his "daddy")* Please stop. Stop yelling at mommy.

And now we actually HEAR it with him. A DOMESTIC QUARREL which worsens quickly. The "dad" is yelling at the "mom," *backing her down, ridiculing her, accusing her, and she fights back verbally. It's a battle of loud booming voices.*

"DAD": *(V.O.)* I don't care what you want, we're going to the Hutman's tonight. No, damn it, get yourself dressed. We're walking out the door in fifteen minutes.

"MOM": *(V.O.)* I'm not going over there again. Sharon was very rude to me last time and...

"DAD": *(V.O.) (interrupting)* She wasn't rude. You're jealous of their home, her cooking, Bud's income...

"MOM": *(V.O.) (interrupting)* That's not fair. You heard what she said to me...

"DAD": *(V.O.) (interrupting)* I've heard enough of this crap. Get into the damn bedroom and put some clothes on. And don't wear that low-topped blouse. It looks sleezy.

And the loud argument continues on under the following.

JIMMY: *(to Clerk)* Make it stop. Please, make it stop.

Jimmy huddles in a ball now, crying hopelessly.

JIMMY: *(cont'd)* Mommy, come here. Come over here Mommy.

CLERK: It's okay Jimmy.

JIMMY: No, he's hurting her. Mommy! He's hurting her.

Jimmy's breathing hard and crying.

CLERK: *(desperately)* Okay, okay, I'll make it stop. *(to "daddy")* Stop it! Shut up! Leave her alone now. You get away from her!

The argument abruptly ends. Jimmy's still crying.

CLERK: *(cont'd) (to Jimmy)* Jimmy, it's okay, she's safe. It's alright now. He's gone. You're okay. Your mom's okay.

Jimmy looks up at the Clerk, who is now his mother.

JIMMY: I love you mommy. I love you so much. Don't let them take you away. Mommy, please don't leave me.

CLERK: I'm right here Jimmy.

JIMMY: I gotta go outside. The sounds, it's my head again. It hurts. It's going so fast. I gotta go.

Time is racing for him now.

JIMMY: *(cont'd)* Make it stop, mommy. It hurts.

CLERK: Okay, okay, let's go outside.

They get up from the bench and walk around a bit.

CLERK: *(cont'd)* Look, it's sunny out. Very nice now. Everything's slowed down. Can you hear, Jimmy? There's birds singing a little song. It's so pretty And I'm right here.

JIMMY: I'm gonna be okay.

She holds him. Cars drive by, and he's distracted by it, holding his head. She calms him.

CLERK: *(in tears now)* I love you, your daddy loves you. Please be okay, Jimmy.

JIMMY: I'll be alright.

They sit down again on the bench. He's in her arms. She strokes his hair. He's calmed down now. People are finally leaving them alone. Cars driving by, sounds of the city are back. Tears dry up. Jimmy finally relaxes, then looks over, but doesn't recognize her.

JIMMY: *(cont'd)* I gotta go.

Jimmy gets up to walk off without his umbrella.

CLERK: *(handing it to him)* Your umbrella.

He takes it and the Clerk returns to her store.

JIMMY: *(turning to his "older sister" Mary)* You can't have all the soda Mary. Leave me some … **Oh!** *(he breaks out laughing)* You spilled it on your head! You're so funny Mary. "Yo ho ho and a bottle of rum." The caps were off! ... Lemme do it too, Mary. Let me.

Jimmy "pours" the soda on his head, laughing and crying as he walks away.

Wiretap

IN AN OFFICE OF THE F.B.I. – *An FBI Agent meets with STEVENS, a female private attorney, in his office at FBI HQ.*

FBI: Oh hi. Listen, thanks for dropping by on a Saturday.

STEVENS: What is it you wanted to talk about?

FBI: Can I get you some coffee?

STEVENS: No thanks. What's this about?

FBI: About one of your clients.

STEVENS: Well, that'd be a pretty one-sided conversation. There's this attorney-client privilege thing, you know.

FBI: Oh, okay.

STEVENS: Anything else I can do for you?

FBI: You could go to prison and lose your license to practice law.

STEVENS: What? ... And how would that work, exactly?

FBI: I think you know the answer to that one, counselor.

Stevens heads to the door to walk out as FBI does paperwork.

STEVENS: Well, I never was much for guessing games.

FBI: *(without looking up)* Anthony Palmetto and a certain attorney-client trust account.

This stops her cold.

STEVENS: That's confidential information!

FBI: Looks like you took the work-ethic a little too far on the Palmetto file.

STEVENS: Is that right?

FBI: As a matter of fact, you're about one step away from being placed under arrest for a RICO violation – conspiracy to launder drug money.

STEVENS: Really? Well I think you're putting your balls in a vice here, Agent Morrissey, attempting to invade the attorney-client relationship over threat of unlawful arrest. And I think the U.S.-fucking-Attorney's Office is gonna fry your tight ass.

FBI: Are you done?

STEVENS: I'll be done when I talk to the U.S. Attorney first thing Monday morning.

FBI: I'll save you the trouble. See, it's the U.S. Attorney who got us the warrant for the wiretap we've got in your law office.

STEVENS: You've got wiretaps in my god damned law office? You slimy fucks!

FBI: *(calmly)* No, I don't think we're the slimy fucks. You crossed the motherfucking line and now we got you, Stevens. ... Are you ready to sit down and be civil?

STEVENS: Yes.

Stevens sits, beginning to see the bigger picture.

FBI: Okay, here's what I figure. I figure you don't want to do fifteen years in Lompoc at this stage of your illustrious career. And I figure you'd probably not have mob clients but for financial pressures, a new marriage, a kid, mortgage, that kinda stuff. Push a woman over the edge, make her do things she might not otherwise do. And I think you probably want to talk to me about money laundering out of your client trust account.

STEVENS: *(beat)* Palmetto asked me to deposit money into the account. That's not a crime. I got a trust account. Interest goes to the State Bar. I made the deposits.

FBI: Two hundred, two hundred-fifty thousand a month?

STEVENS: That's the way he wanted it. It was his money. I was holding it in trust while...until...

FBI: *(interjecting)* Until Palmetto told you to jump, and how high. And when he wanted the money moved, you moved it. And the ten thousand dollar reporting limit, well the bank just reports it as an attorney-client trust fund transfer. Is that pretty much it?

STEVENS: Okay, but I don't know anything else. Transfers were always to different accounts, different entities. I didn't keep records. That's all I know. I don't even know what business he's...

FBI: *(interrupting)* **Don't paint us the fools**, Stevens. We know how it worked. We got the god damned wiretap, remember? You been snorting too much coke counselor? Now listen up, 'cause you're right on the edge of fuckin' up big time. Help yourself now. It's your play.

Stevens is boxed in, mentally racing over the details of what might have been revealed in the wiretapped conversations, desperate to find a way out.

STEVENS: I, ah, okay, let me just think about this for a minute. ... Could I have a glass of water?

FBI walks away to pour her one.

FBI: *(casually)* Sure...By the way, how's that daughter of yours doing? What's her name, Heather? She's six years old now, so that'd make her about, what? Fourteen or so by the time you got out of Lompoc. 'Course that's if you get "good-time" credits. You...they'd probably put you in lock-down—protect you from predators in the Joint. Something goes bad and there's no good-time credits...*(overlapping begins)*...so that'd bump it up another three or four years...

STEVENS: *(overlapping, worried)* You said, "help yourself" That's what you said. Help myself how?

FBI: Give us what we need to take down Palmetto and his crew.

STEVENS: I can't do that.

FBI: Then as far as I know, you're the main deal. You take the fall.

It's really closing in on her now.

STEVENS: *(pause)* What wiretap evidence do you have?

FBI pulls out the thick wiretap transcripts, tabbed to the good stuff.

FBI: Well, we got you advising Palmetto there all about offshore accounts...secret multi-national deposit transactions...Oh, here's a good one, remember this call? "Dummy corporations to generate the income, false creditors to siphon off the excess cash." (Makes for pretty good reading.) You know, you kinda... map it out for him. Other than that...

STEVENS: And you want me to testify against my client?

FBI sidles close in on his prey.

FBI: No, absolutely not. Not now at least. See, we just want you to vouch for one of our guys. You know, bring him into the fold with Palmetto. And then, it's business as usual. You just keep doin' what you're doin' practicing law, sendin' out the bills, you know, like nothing's changed.

Stevens sees her and her family's lives flash before her eyes. It can't be happening. There's no way out and this is beyond hope. Even her daughter's life is in jeopardy.

STEVENS: *(losing it, emotionally)* Those motherfuckers will kill me! They will hunt me down, I'm telling you. You don't know. They're big. It's not one guy we're talking here, he's just the contact. It's a fucking monster fuck of a criminal enterprise. I put your man in, VOUCH for him? I'm dead. My family's dead. Do you hear me god damn it?! Oh shit, do not do this to me, please. You cannot do this.

FBI: *(pause)* You did this to yourself counselor. We'll be in touch.

FBI walks out with his jacket.

www.ingramcontent.com/pod-product-compliance
Lightning Source LLC
Chambersburg PA
CBHW050633300426
44112CB00012B/1783